In the Spirit of

St. Francis
&
the Sultan

In the Spirit of
St. Francis
&
the Sultan

*Catholics and Muslims
Working Together for the Common Good*

GEORGE DARDESS
AND
MARVIN L. KRIER MICH

ORBIS BOOKS
Maryknoll, New York 10545

Founded in 1970, Orbis Books endeavors to publish works that enlighten the mind, nourish the spirit, and challenge the conscience. The publishing arm of the Maryknoll Fathers and Brothers, Orbis seeks to explore the global dimensions of the Christian faith and mission, to invite dialogue with diverse cultures and religious traditions, and to serve the cause of reconciliation and peace. The books published reflect the views of their authors and do not represent the official position of the Maryknoll Society. To learn more about Maryknoll and Orbis Books, please visit our website at www.maryknollsociety.org.

Copyright © 2011 by George Dardess and Marvin Krier Mich.

Published by Orbis Books, Maryknoll, New York 10545-0302.

All rights reserved.

No part of this publication may be reproduced or transmitted in any form or by any means, electronic or mechanical, including photocopying, recording, or any information storage or retrieval system, without prior permission in writing from the publisher.

All translations of the Qur'an are by Geoge Dardess (except when appearing within quotations by others). Unless otherwise noted all translations of the Bible are from the New Revised Standard Version, copyright © 1993 by the Division of Christian Education of the National Council of the Churches of Christ in the U.S.A. Used by permission. All rights reserved.

Queries regarding rights and permissions should be addressed to
Orbis Books, P.O. Box 302, Maryknoll, NY 10545-0302.

Manufactured in the United States of America.

Library of Congress Cataloging-in-Publication Data

Dardess, George.
    In the spirit of St. Francis and the Sultan : Catholics and Muslims working together for the common good / George Dardess and Marvin L. Krier Mich.
      p. cm.
    Includes bibliographical references and index.
    ISBN 978-1-57075-907-9 (pbk. : alk. paper)
    1. Islam – Relations – Christianity. 2. Christianity and other religions – Islam. 3. Religious pluralism – Islam. 4. Religious pluralism – Christianity. I. Mich, Marvin L. Krier. II. Title. III. Title: In the spirit of Saint Francis and the Sultan. IV. Title: Catholics and Muslims working together for the common good.
    BP172.D37235 2011
    261.2′7 – dc22
                                          2010032347

*—strive together as in a race
to do works of justice....*
— Qur'an Sura al-Ma'idah 5:48

*"Which of these three, in your opinion,
was neighbor to the man who fell in with the robbers?
the Priest, the Levite, or the Samaritan?"
The answer came, "The Samaritan,
the one who treated him with compassion."
Jesus said to him, "Then go and do the same."*
— Gospel of Luke 11:36–37

CONTENTS

Part II

REVIEWING EACH OTHER'S
SCRIPTURAL WARRANTS
FOR SOCIAL JUSTICE MINISTRY

Part III

GREETING THE ANGELS
(AS WELL AS CONFRONTING THE DEMONS)
OF OUR HISTORICAL RELATIONSHIP

PREFACE:
AN OFFERING OF THANKS

Our first thank you goes to Timo Jackle, of Rochester, New York. Timo, at the time a participant in a JustFaith program at Rochester's Blessed Sacrament Church, was attending a presentation on Muslim-Christian dialogue held at Rochester's Islamic Center. Both of the future authors of this book were present. Timo asked us afterward, "Why isn't there a JustFaith program for Christians and Muslims?" The authors looked at each other and replied, almost in unison, "That's a great idea!"

And so the seed for this book was planted. But it could not have grown without the support of the national organization that created the JustFaith program, JustFaith Ministries. JustFaith Ministries, guided by Jack Jezreel, writes curricula for building small Christian communities dedicated to social justice outreach. Timo's inspiration was the direct result of the effectiveness of the JustFaith program in inspiring its participants to imagine fresh new applications of social justice principles.

Guiding groups within a particular religion or religious denomination to form social justice–oriented communities is, of course, not a new idea. While various guides for such groups have been produced, the guides created by JustFaith appear to be among the most successful. JustFaith Ministries has won the support of Catholic Charities, the Catholic Campaign for Human Development, Catholic Relief Services, Bread for the World, Maryknoll Fathers and Brothers, and Pax Christi USA. JustFaith has also produced a version of its program for ecumenical Christian groups.

We have been much inspired by the JustFaith model. One of this book's writers has even written a text (*The Challenge and*

Spirituality of Catholic Social Teaching) specifically designed for use by JustFaith groups, and both of us have facilitated JustFaith programs at our respective parishes. On the strength of our positive experience with the JustFaith model, we have shaped our book as a first-of-its-kind guide for a JustFaith style interfaith gathering involving Christians and Muslims. Shorter in duration than the JustFaith program and modeled after JustFaith's JustMatters format (normally encompassing eight meetings instead of Just-Faith's thirty), the gathering we envision, and for which we hope to provide guidance, would nevertheless incorporate most of Just-Faith's key elements: prayer, community-building, study of each religion's scriptures and social justice traditions, and the planning of actions to promote the common good.

But while our book envisions usage by JustFaith ministries, it is not restricted to such use. We have planned it in such a way that all Christians, whether familiar with JustFaith or not, can feel at home in it. We hope that Muslims will feel at home in it too. Both Christians and Muslims must feel that they are being treated as equals in our book and that no advantage has been given to either group by the authors' own religious orientations or past experiences. We have done all in our power to make such evenhandedness a reality.

Yet even the guidance of JustFaith Ministries would not have been enough if the authors didn't live in a city, Rochester, New York, whose resources for ecumenical and interfaith dialogue weren't among the most developed and creative in the country. For example, the accord signed between Roman Catholic Bishop Matthew Clark and the Masajid (Mosques) of Rochester on May 5, 2003, was the first of its kind in the United States and perhaps in the world. Bishop Clark had signed a similar accord with the Jewish communities of Rochester on May 8, 1996, and with the Episcopal Church of Rochester a few years before that on May 22, 1988. The signers of all three accords pledged to work in solidarity to oppose prejudice and to strive together for the common good.

In addition, the Greater Rochester Community of Churches (GRCC), founded in 1909, is an ecumenical coalition of churches that enthusiastically works with all religious traditions. Again, the common theme is service to others, especially to victims of prejudice and marginalization. A more recent arrival among Rochester communities promoting interfaith dialogue is Nazareth College's nationally recognized Center for Interfaith Study and Dialogue (CISD), led by Dr. Muhammad Shafiq, past imam of Rochester's Islamic Center. Dr. Shafiq is a leader among American imams working toward ecumenism within their own ranks and toward interfaith dialogue with non-Muslims.

Both of us have benefited immeasurably from our associations with many of the groups mentioned above. One of us, Dr. Dardess, studied Arabic and the Qur'an at the Islamic Center under Dr. Shafiq's guidance. And both of us have sought to express our gratitude both by service on various committees of these groups and by leadership. (Dr. Dardess is a member of Rochester's Commission on Muslim-Christian Relations as well as of the Muslim-Catholic Alliance; Dr. Mich is current president of the GRCC.) Without such a broad and vibrant community of interfaith effort surrounding and encouraging us, we would never have had the confidence to respond to the challenge of a book like the present one.

Much of the challenge of our book lay in deciding how to focus it for our Muslim and Christian readers. Was there a common symbol of interfaith action that both religious communities could identify with? We found that symbol in the meeting between St. Francis and Sultan Malik al-Kamil at Damietta in 1219. Two people in particular brought the meeting to our attention, so thanks is due them both: Sister Kathy Warren, OSF, associate producer of the Damietta Project, a three-part video resource (in process) for use by groups exploring religious diversity both for mutual enrichment and for the strength with which to build a peaceful society; and Professor Paul Moses, author of *The Saint and the Sultan: The Crusades, Islam, and Francis of Assisi's Mission of Peace* (New York: Doubleday, 2009). We were captivated

by Sr. Kathy's and Professor Moses's characterization of Francis
as a peacemaker to the enemy Other, the hated Saracen whom
the pope's armies were besieging at Damietta, Egypt, during the
Fifth Crusade. We were inspired in our own book to use elements
of Professor Moses's presentation of both Francis and the Sultan
as peacemakers as a way of encouraging contemporary Muslims
and Christians to follow in their footsteps. The example of Francis and the Sultan points the way for all of us to travel as we come
together amid comparable tension and violence to work for the
common good.

We make clear in our book that our vision of Francis and
the Sultan as peacemakers is the preferred interpretation based
on the facts available to us. There exists no eye-witness account
of the two men's conversations in the Sultan's tent outside
Damietta. Contemporary accounts are secondhand and reflect
obvious biases. As a result, we can accept in part the conclusion of
Professor John Tolan's *Saint Francis and the Sultan: The Curious
History of a Christian-Muslim Encounter:* "Each interpreter reads
into [the] encounter his or her own preoccupations."[1] Professor
Tolan does not mention the book of Professor Moses, but very
likely he would judge it as he does the many similar accounts pre-
ceding Moses as a well-meaning but misguided effort to fill in the
empty spaces of the factual record. He would see Moses's interpretation as but an elaboration of then Cardinal Joseph Ratzinger's
(now Pope Benedict) in 2002: a characterization of Francis as
an opponent of the Crusades and as a minister of peace to the
Sultan. "Let us walk down the path toward peace, following the
example of Saint Francis,"[2] exhorted Cardinal Ratzinger. In Professor Tolan's view, Professor Moses's interpretation of events, like
the pope's, would be just as unreliable as earlier accounts reflecting an opposite bias, in which the Crusades are ordained by God
and in which Francis spiritually vanquishes Islam by cowing the
Sultan and his followers.

Ironically, however, Professor Tolan cannot escape creating
an interpretation of his own. It is a very bleak, discouraging
one. "Beyond these fragmentary sources, the historian gazes into

emptiness and admits his ignorance."[3] But we might ask, Why bother to pursue the question of what Damietta might mean for humanity if the result leads to so little — to mere "emptiness"? Perhaps the historian's role has its limitations, just as it has when pursuing the wraith of the "historical Jesus." Ultimately, faith and imagination must be enlisted in the search for truth. To expect hard facts alone, important as they are, to guide us to human flourishing is to expect too much of those facts.

For precisely there lies our antidote to Professor Tolan's "emptiness"; its source is in "human flourishing." This is the concept (expressed variously as the common good, or *shalom,* or *salaam*) we bring to our interpretation of such facts as we have about the meeting between Francis and the Sultan. We eagerly seek to know if those facts can support such a concept, even while knowing that they can be interpreted otherwise, even in an opposite sense. An example of such an interpretation can be found in Frank M. Rega's *St. Francis of Assisi and the Conversion of the Muslims.*[4] Rega's book echoes some of the trumphalist readings of Francis's encounter that were common in earlier centuries. Such readings promote the question to ask about this or similar books: To what extent do their authors identify their own biases? For we who study the sources of the encounter between Francis and the Sultan are all to some degree, as Professor Tolan shows, looking into "a distant mirror . . . in which, over the centuries, each observer perceives only the reflection of his own fears and hopes."[5]

We, the writers of this book, confess to bias only with respect to the specific details of the encounter itself, and for the reason already stated: lack of an absolutely reliable eyewitness report. Thanks to the hard work of Sister Kathy Warren, Paul Moses, and others, however, the main intentions of both Francis and the Sultan to strive for peace and mutual understanding within the tent of meeting at Damietta have come into clear focus. That clarity allows us to derive hope for human flourishing even through the dimness of the historical record and amid the gloom of the Muslim-Christian tensions of our own time.

A Note on "Gendered" Language for God

Readers will note that throughout our book we occasionally use capitalized forms of the masculine pronoun (He, Him, His) when referring to God. We do this in deference to Muslim custom and belief. The equivalent of the name "God" in Arabic, the language of the Qur'an, is Allah, a noun considered masculine only in grammatical form, not in gender. Allah (God) is beyond gender and beyond even being, because Allah (God) is the Creator of gender and being. Accordingly, Muslims strictly avoid all gendered language for God. For example, Muslims do not call God "Father." To use such a name would, according to Muslim belief, detract from God's absolute majesty. Capitalizing the masculine pronouns used for God ("He" rather than "he") highlights that majesty.

INTRODUCTION

The World Today

At the beginning of this twenty-first century, what kind of world do Americans live in? Does anything seem to resemble the world of our grandparents or parents? Or have there been drastic changes all around us?

These questions hardly need asking. It would be difficult to find any American who thinks the world has been standing still over the last few decades. Quite the contrary! Change is everywhere, in America's physical environment, in its economy, in its workplaces, and in its neighborhoods.

Let's look a little closer at changes in those neighborhoods. No longer can Americans assume that our neighbors go to the same church that we attend, or go to church at all, or that they belong to Americans' "own" Christian faith tradition. Our "neighborhood" of today may consist of growing numbers of Muslims, Jews, Buddhists, or Hindus. Our neighbors may come from the Midwest or the South or Mexico or Iran or India or Korea. Often Americans greet these proofs of their increasing diversity with interest and enthusiasm. The diversity delivers them from stagnation and complacency. But Americans also react to such changes with fear. The diversity seems to threaten the social order we treasure.

It even seems at times to threaten our very lives.

This threat becomes especially vivid to Americans when we think about Islam and Muslims. A test of the high anxiety Islam and Muslims arouse in Americans is to notice the way we react to the following unfinished statement: "If Christians and Muslims are not at peace. . . ."

How are Americans today likely to finish that sentence? Don't we do so with a shudder? Don't we hear ourselves adding words like the following: "then it's possible the whole world will end up in flames!" "September 11 will seem like a brushfire!"?

Why do Americans tend to react to the possibility of Christians and Muslims *not* being at peace with such grim, panicky foreboding? Isn't this an odd state of affairs? At least it's a very recent one. September 11, 2001, really does seem to mark a seismic shift in the way Americans imagine relations between Christians and Muslims and especially the consequence of those relations.

Consider the implications for human flourishing of the following findings and statistics:

- "Public attitudes about Muslims and Islam have grown more negative in recent years."[1]

- "When asked for the single word that best describes their impression of Islam, far more Americans mention negative words than positive words (30 percent vs. 15 percent)."[2]

- "Many Americans harbor fears that the terrorist attacks of recent years are indicative of an existing or imminent major world conflict between the West and Islam."[3]

- "Most Muslims and Westerners are convinced that relations between them are generally bad these days. Many in the West see Muslims as fanatical, violent, and as lacking tolerance. Meanwhile, Muslims in the Middle East and Asia generally see Westerners as selfish, immoral, and greedy — as well as violent and fanatical."[4]

These findings reveal the negative attitudes toward Muslims and Islam that are pervasive in the American non-Muslim population — attitudes that have been growing in strength. The tragic events of September 11, 2001, and the ensuing "War on Terror" have signaled in some quarters an inevitable "clash of civilizations" between the West and the world's one billion, three hundred million Muslims. The fact that many millions of Muslims make their homes in the West has only seemed to deepen suspicion of those who hold and practice Islam. Many influential figures in Western governments, media, universities, and religious institutions continue to assert that Islam is an inherently violent religion and that espousing it entails terrorist behavior and an insidious program of world domination (for example, the return and victory of the Caliphate over the nations of the West).

The findings above also show the corresponding negative attitudes particularly of Middle Eastern and Asian Muslims toward Westerners. These mirroring negative attitudes — and the fears that underlie them — make a dangerous combination in our world. They may actually incite the "major world conflict between the West and Islam" that we fear.

We all, Muslims and non-Muslims alike, have a choice. Either we allow our fears to bear us along toward what could eventually become a war of apocalyptic dimensions. Or we can rouse ourselves from our fearful obsessions and search for ways not only to reverse this negative trend but also, and most importantly, to focus the world's energies on achieving peace and human flourishing.

Do faithful Christians and Muslims have a role to play in this positive, life-enhancing mission? The question answers itself. The God of both Christians and Muslims, the one God, has given both communities two commandments that override all their differences: to love God and to serve their neighbor, especially the neighbor who is poor or marginalized. Groups of faithful Christians and Muslims living out these commandments by working in solidarity with each other could set an example others in their communities would follow. And not only others in their own communities, but others in all other communities, both religious and secular. If that were to happen, then the positive form of our heading above would have force. It would read "If Christians and Muslims are at peace..." and what we would be talking about would be the beginning of a social transformation benefiting everyone.

Some First Steps toward Peace

Muslim scholars underlined the urgency of Christian-Muslim solidarity with their groundbreaking document published in 2007 titled *A Common Word between Us and You*. Addressed to the world's Christian communities, but in a particular way (for reasons we will discuss in chapter 7) to Pope Benedict himself, the document asserts:

> Finding common ground between Muslims and Christians is not simply a matter for polite ecumenical dialogue between selected religious leaders. Christianity and Islam are the largest and second largest religions in the world and in history. Christians and Muslims reportedly make up over a third and over a fifth of humanity respectively. Together they make up more than 55 percent of the world's population, making the relationship between these two religious communities the most important factor in contributing to meaningful peace around the world. *If Muslims and Christians are not at peace, the world cannot be at peace.*[5]

Pope Benedict responded to the "A Common Word" document by inviting the scholars to the Vatican for a seminar inaugurating the Catholic-Muslim Forum. In his welcoming speech Pope Benedict affirmed the urgency of both communities' working together in the cause of defending human dignity:

> Only by starting with the recognition of the centrality of the person and the dignity of each human being, respecting and defending life which is the gift of God, and is thus sacred for Christians and for Muslims alike — only on the basis of this recognition, can we find a common ground for building a more fraternal world, a world in which confrontations and differences are peacefully settled, and the devastating power of ideologies is neutralized.[6]

One danger of interfaith seminars is that they can easily turn into "feel-good" gatherings involving elites. Statements urging our common humanity can end up sounding like pious common-places. The language of both the Muslim scholars and the pope recognizes this danger and works to counteract it. Note Pope Benedict's use of the word "building" in the phrase "building a more fraternal world." Note too the Muslim scholars' observation that "finding common ground between Muslims and Christians is not simply a matter for polite ecumenical dialogue between selected religious leaders." What both the pope and the scholars are calling for involves not only discussion but also risk and hard work — risk and hard work to be accepted by all Christians and Muslims, not just by the leadership. All adherents of the two religions, from the most powerful and learned to the least, have a role to play in "building a more fraternal world."

Pope Benedict makes this point explicit elsewhere in his welcoming speech:

> The great interest which the present Seminar has awakened is an incentive for us to ensure that the reflections and the positive developments which emerge from Muslim-Christian dialogue are not limited to a small group of experts and scholars, but are passed on as a precious legacy to be placed at the service of all, to bear fruit in the way we live each day.[7]

The stakes of interfaith dialogue have become such that common ground has to be sought — and won — by Christians and Muslims working at all levels. The divide between the two faiths cannot be bridged, nor the work in solidarity for the common good be initiated, unless the grassroots become as involved in dialogue as the elites. Benedict eventually went further, asserting in later writings that the most urgently needed interreligious dialogue at the moment isn't theological, but practical and cultural. This kind of dialogue requires everyone's assistance, not just that of learned experts.

The pope made the point with special force during a speech at his January 17, 2010, visit to the Great Synagogue of Rome. He began by proposing the Torah as the basis of a "great ethical code" for humanity, one that would lead Jews and Catholics into "areas of cooperation and witness." The pope then gave a list of those areas: resisting secularism by "reawakening in our society openness to the transcendent dimension"; defending the right to life and the family; promoting justice for "the poor, women and children, strangers, the sick, the weak and the needy"; and acting on behalf of peace, especially peace in the Holy Land. In his report on this event, John Allen pointed out that "all this amounts to an application of what Benedict has described as a shift from 'inter-religious' to 'inter-cultural' dialogue." Allen then refers us to a book introduction in which Benedict wrote:

> Interreligious dialogue in the strict sense of the term is not possible without putting one's own faith into parentheses, while intercultural dialogue that develops the cultural consequences of the religious option . . . is both possible and urgent.[8]

While Benedict was addressing Judaism and Jews in his Great Synagogue speech, his words apply equally appropriately to Muslims and Islam. The business of the great religions is to heal the world, not endlessly to elaborate their theological differences. As a gifted theologian himself, Pope Benedict is not disparaging theology. He is saying that what Vatican II called the "signs of the times" requires a joining of hands and hearts by the great religions in order to address overwhelming challenges to the very survival of the created order.

Who Is the Audience for This Book?

In the Spirit of St. Francis and the Sultan is designed for the grassroots: for the laity, not for theologians and experts in interfaith dialogue.

At the same time, *In the Spirit of St. Francis and the Sultan* is not a "top-down" book, one that lays out prescriptions for others at a "lower" level to follow. Rather, we, the authors, try to speak to the grassroots directly, as members of the grassroots ourselves.

We speak in a tone that is calm and easy-going (without becoming loose or casual). We do so because we are convinced that the tension and grimness characterizing many current discussions of Muslim-Christian relations perpetuate a hopeless sense of doom about an inevitable, dire "clash of civilizations." We are convinced, too, that joy is at the heart of both these faiths, and that the positive, constructive behavior both faiths inspire expresses this core creative confidence in a God who desires our mutual flourishing or *salaam*. That is why we suggest, share, recommend, rather than insist, proclaim, dictate. We base our recommendations not on theoretical models but on lessons we've learned from our own experience as facilitators of interfaith dialogue. These lessons are always focused concretely on the various rewards and pitfalls accompanying Muslims and Christians as they walk the path toward solidarity. We try as much as possible to divert attention away from ourselves as this book's authors and to direct it instead to those Christians and Muslims who are taking their courageous first step of gathering for the common good.

Since much if not all of the distrust between Christians and Muslims results from ignorance, we start right out with an introduction to the religion of the Other. Of course, no complete presentation of Christianity or Islam is possible in a book as brief as this. We believe, however, that it is possible even in a short book for both groups to grasp the essentials of each other's religion. We believe also that it is possible to write and talk about each religion in a way that is engaging for its adherents and also accessible for those unfamiliar to it. We try to do justice to the facts of both religions, especially in their social justice dimensions. But we don't try to be exhaustive. We believe we can count on the Christians and Muslims who use this book to amplify what we say for the benefit of their counterparts in faith. We hope our book will provide group members, whether Christian or Muslim, with a "teaching opportunity," so that members of one faith will fill in the inevitable gaps in our presentation for the benefit of the others. Such peer teaching will strengthen the bonds of solidarity our book intends to encourage.

The benefit of our "adult-centered" learning model is that it empowers participants to reflect on their own experience and knowledge of being Christian or Muslim — even if their knowledge is imperfect or partial — and to play the roles of both tutors and learners with their interfaith partners. More specifically, the approach empowers adults to take responsibility for their understanding of their faith and to articulate and share this understanding with members of the other faith tradition. It also empowers adults to be open to understanding the faith of their dialogue partner.

We hope by these means to guide Christians and Muslims to an understanding of the common ground their faith traditions share, which is "the dignity of each human being, respecting and defending life which is the gift of God." This common ground will become the solid basis for action in solidarity for the common good.

Our approach, empowering the grassroots, is, as far as we can tell, the first of its kind in books urging Christian-Muslim dialogue. Our approach complements more formal levels of interfaith dialogue already occurring in academic and religious settings. We hope our book will help support and even strengthen dialogue on those more formal levels by widening the audience for it and by encouraging dialogue on all levels, whether among the elites or at the grassroots, to focus concretely on "building a more fraternal world."

Where Do We Start?

The place to begin is not very complicated. The place to begin is with Christians and Muslims actually gathering in the same space to get to know each other.

Uncomplicated as this precondition sounds, it is not so easy to achieve. It requires both Christians and Muslims to get out of their so-called "comfort zones." These comfort zones are rather like suits of armor. Constructed out of the various fears and prejudices that Christians tend to have about Muslims and that Muslims tend to have about Christians, this armor becomes so thick that those taking shelter behind it lose contact with reality. As a result, they become incapable of opening themselves to the "enemy" on any level, whether physically, psychologically, or spiritually.

Research identifies two factors that lead non-Muslims to throw off their armor and, on doing so, to begin to develop more positive attitudes toward Muslims. These factors are: *knowledge* of Islam and a *personal acquaintance* with a Muslim. A Pew Forum report gives this finding:

> Among Americans with little knowledge of Islam, fewer than half express favorable views of Muslim-Americans. By contrast, among Americans who are relatively more knowledgeable about Islam, more than six-in-ten express positive views.

The report continues:

> Finally, there is a strong relationship between personal acquaintance with a Muslim and views of Muslim-Americans. Among those who say they personally know someone who is a Muslim, 74 percent have a positive impression of Muslim-Americans, compared with only 50 percent of those who do not personally know any Muslims.[9]

Comparable data doesn't exist for Muslim Americans, since as a minority within a Christian-dominant society Muslim Americans are very aware of Christians. They deal with them daily. But Muslim-Americans also suffer, as Christians do, from negative attitudes toward the Other. This negativity results not so much from ignorance as from feelings of exclusion and alienation. According to polling of Muslim-Americans by CAIR in 2006, 43 percent answered affirmatively to the question, "Have you ever felt discriminated against or profiled?"[10] While the intensity of the fear each has for the other might be similar, the nature of the fear is different. For American non-Muslims, it's the fear of terrorism; for American Muslims, it's the fear of scapegoating and rejection. Either way, both Christians and Muslims have to emerge from their "comfort zones" in order to *see* each other, perhaps for the first time, for what they are: loved equally by their Creator God and enjoined equally by that God to serve God's creation.

But even when they decide they want to emerge from their armor the groups have trouble finding each other. This is a problem particularly for Christians. Christians sometimes claim: "But I don't *know* any Muslims. I doubt that there's a single Muslim within a hundred miles of here!" Chances are, though, that there are many American Muslims living close to Christians who speak this way, even in rural parts of the United States. American Muslims' threatened minority status often makes them unwilling to identify themselves publicly. And parochial attitudes on the part of some Christians make it hard for them to know their neighbors on any but a superficial level. In this situation, Christians and Muslims should consult local interfaith groups for contact information about possible interfaith partners. Fortunately, an increasing number of such groups has been springing up in recent years. It ought to be possible, except in remote areas, for interfaith-minded Christians to find interfaith-minded Muslims, and vice versa.

And Where Are We Headed?

The goal of *In the Spirit of St. Francis and the Sultan* involves more than cultivating positive attitudes, however. While cultivating positive attitudes is essential for overcoming the negativity revealed in the Pew Forum's findings, positive attitudes aren't ends in themselves. Positive attitudes are preconditions for fulfilling the roles our respective religions enjoin upon us (our becoming Creation's "stewards" in the Christian tradition, God's *khalifa,* or "trustees," in the Islamic). Positive attitudes are also byproducts of our concrete efforts to transform unjust practices and structures. Positive attitudes aren't abstract moral ideals or intellectual achievements. They are the fruits of communal effort toward a goal that benefits all humanity.

For that is where we are heading: toward building the "more fraternal world" Pope Benedict speaks about. Yes, Christian-Muslim work in solidarity will require mutual confidence-building. It will require acquaintance with each other's scriptures, histories, and traditions as well. But the goal of the collaboration will be the identification and implementation of concrete steps to address the needs of the greater community, especially those needs caused by systemic injustice: poverty, racism, environmental damage, and the like. Our book will guide mixed groups of Muslims and Christians to reach that goal. They will move through an eight-step process, following our eight-chapter format. During the eight-step process they will learn from each other, dispel mutual misunderstandings, face together the convenient and not-so-convenient truths of their intertwining history, and, finally, roll up their sleeves to build a world in which — again quoting Pope Benedict — "confrontations and differences are peacefully settled, and the devastating power of ideologies is neutralized."

Yes, Maybe, but What Do You Mean by "Interfaith Dialogue"?

"Dialogue" has become such a trendy word that our using it so often might seem a discouraging sign. There's reason to feel that way. As commonly used, "dialogue" tends to refer to two extremes of dealing politely with your rivals: at one extreme, it refers to arguing with them without raising your voice and, at the other, to just palling around with them in a show of bonhomie. Considered in this light, "dialogue" can at best promise only to soften the effects of rivalry. It cannot cure it.

Yet the word has more value than that. "Dialogue" is handy as shorthand for peaceful, productive interaction between groups that have a historical tendency to treat each other dismissively and even aggressively. Genuine dialogue means at the very least attentiveness to the Other's views. Dialogue means listening to those views patiently rather than jumping to conclusions about them or about those who hold them; it means resisting stereotypes of the Other rather than succumbing to them. The goal of genuine dialogue is the solution of the issues that caused the rivalry in the first place.

But even this understanding of dialogue falls short. Dialogue involves more than conscious intention, however benign. It is more than a technique. Dialogue assumes a strong desire first to resist the intoxications of rivalry and then to seek in its place a deeper reality that can nurture a truly constructive attitude toward the Other. We can speak of that deeper reality as a state of spiritual centeredness that actually precedes dialogue and makes dialogue possible.

The French Jewish philosopher Emmanuel Levinas can be our guide here. Already for him, many years ago, "dialogue" was a compromised term, little more than a feel-good word for the exchanges between estranged groups that had no real intention of understanding each other. That's why he entitled an important speech he gave in 1947 "Beyond Dialogue." He wanted to encourage a truly fluid exchange between "others." And though in 1947 Levinas was thinking about exchanges between Jews and Christians, what he said then applies just as well to dialogue — or what is "beyond dialogue" — between Christians and Muslims today.[11]

Levinas believed that when previously estranged groups go beyond superficial dialogue, their rivalrous relationships dissolve. But even more: the dissolution reveals the true state of affairs between them that the rivalry has covered up, a state of mutual need and responsibility. According to Levinas, our fundamental relationship to each other is not predatory. What Hobbes, quoting the Roman playwright Plautus, said about human nature — *homo lupus homini* (man is a wolf to man) — is not true. Fundamentally we are related as healers of each other's hurts and inadequacies.

But fear makes us resist admitting such weaknesses. Fear causes us to put up barriers to the Other, even to prey upon him (or her). That's why Levinas says that "To go toward the Other" leads us directly to "that place from which, for an insufficiently mature soul, hatred flows naturally or is deduced with infallible logic."

What can we do? There is only one solution: risk. The very encounter where the "wolf" in us emerges is the same place where the lamb dwells. We have to enter directly into the wolf's mouth of our own broken human nature in order to escape the wolf, or rather to tame him, turn him into the lamb. That same radical difference we experience in each other (what Levinas calls our "alterity") can cause either violence or mutual growth in self-understanding, depending on whether our soul is "sufficiently mature."

So dialogue doesn't mean avoiding the Other's differences or tip-toeing around him or her or secretly persuading the Other to give those differences up. A "sufficiently mature" soul, with God's help, is able to move beyond such double-dealing. Dialogue means a deeply nondefensive engagement with the Other in exploring those very differences, trusting that our mutual openness to each other, if intelligently and sensitively handled, will bring us both to the healing we need.

Since Vatican II, the Catholic Church has given a lot of thought to interfaith dialogue in the sense in which Levinas and other philosophers have defined it. One fruit of this thinking has been insight into the various forms in which true dialogue might occur between people of different faiths. For example, in the document "Dialogue and Proclamation" issued by the Pontifical Council for Inter-Religious Dialogue, the writers see interreligious dialogue as a "sharing of life" on all levels among those engaged in it. They then break the idea of dialogue down into four aspects, not privileging one aspect over the other, but saying rather that interfaith dialogue isn't fulfilled unless all four are active:

1. First there's the "dialogue of life," where "people [of different faiths] strive to live in an open and neighborly spirit, sharing their joys and sorrows, their human problems and preoccupations."

2. Second there's the "dialogue of action," where "Christians and others collaborate for the integral development and liberation of people."

3. Third is the "dialogue of theological exchange," where "specialists seek to deepen their understanding of their respective religious heritages and to appreciate each other's spiritual values."

4. Fourth is the "dialogue of religious experience," where "persons, rooted in their own religious traditions, share their spiritual riches, for instance with regard to prayer and contemplation, faith and ways of searching for God or the Absolute."[12]

In this book, we'll focus on three of these aspects of interfaith dialogue: on the dialogues of life, of action, and of religious experience. While the dialogue of action is our explicit focus, we know that it cannot be isolated from the other two, from the dialogues of life and of religious experience. Collaborating on projects for the common good will bear little fruit if it is not sustained by openness to and respect for each other's ways of living and if it isn't also deepened by a sharing in each other's spirituality, even though there will inevitably be differences, some of them puzzling and even painfully contradictory, in our respective religious beliefs. As for the dialogue of theological exchange, none of us (it is assumed) will have the expertise to take part in it directly. But it would be helpful for groups that have already gone through the process we're outlining here and have reached a high comfort level with each other to attend conferences where the dialogue of study is featured or to invite religious scholars from both faiths to come speak to them. Input of this kind, coming at the right moment in a group's development, can add greatly to a group's self-understanding.

The final point to be made about dialogue is that it requires both patience and respect for the process itself. Often people with a strong calling to social justice want to jump right into the dialogue of action. They acknowledge the value of the dialogues of life and of religious experience, but find the world's problems too pressing to allow them the luxury of delay. "Let's get to it!" they say. "Time for get-togethers and prayer later, when we need a break." Their eagerness is commendable, but also self-limiting. The work for the common good this book is urging must be done by human hands, true. But the work is God's, not ours — both Catholics and Muslims can agree on that much without a lot of discussion. And God enlists our whole persons, not just our hands, in God's effort to bring God's created world to fullness of being or *salaam*. Whole persons require time and experience to develop through relationship with God and each other. Dialogue can't be rushed. It has its own rhythm and pacing. All that follows in this book is simply a plan to respect that pacing, so that when groups do reach the dialogue of action, they'll find themselves fully prepared for it. And the work of their hands will be that much more effective.

Our Book's Plan in More Detail

In the Spirit of St. Francis and the Sultan has a four-part structure.

In Part I, "Building Confidence," we suggest ways that Christians and Muslims can see each other, not as stereotypes but as human beings created by the one God whom both groups worship and seek to serve. We provide selected scriptural texts from both traditions, pointing out key commonalties and presenting key divergences that will not confuse or alienate group members of the other religion. Our aim is for all group members to focus on beliefs held in common (such as the Oneness of God, the mission of Abraham and the Prophets) and to accept with patience and humility non-negotiable differences (for example, Jesus as God, the Trinity).

Part II, "Reviewing Each Other's Warrants in Scripture and Tradition for Social Justice Ministry," highlights the centrality of social justice in both Christian and Muslim scripture and tradition. Our approach is rooted in Roman Catholic social teaching, but it is not meant to exclude other understandings of social justice in the Christian churches. We encourage the entire group to explore similarities and differences in their conception of the basis of social justice. We stress that social justice for both groups is not an abstract "add-on" to faith but a constituent part of it, an orientation exemplified in the teachings of both Jesus and Muhammad and profoundly embodied in their lives and behavior.

In Part III, "Greeting the Angels (as Well as Confronting the Demons) of Our Historical Relationship," we take a bold step. We assume that the group members have by now overcome their initial fears and suspicions of each other and have begun to grasp their great commonalties. Trusting in their progress, we now encourage a step that might have defeated them earlier. We encourage them to explore some of the key stages of their shared history. While this history contains deplorable events (the Crusades, September 11) and attitudes (racism, xenophobia), it also contains the record of mutual benefits, through cross-fertilization in the arts, in science, in philosophy, and even in religion (as exemplified, as we will shortly describe, in the meeting of Francis and the Sultan).

Finally, in Part IV, "Working in Solidarity for the *Salaam* of the Kingdom," we return to the social justice emphasis of Part II, this time for the purpose of identifying social justice principles the group can hold in common and can use in formulating specific projects for building the common good.

Using This Book

While we make specific suggestions throughout our book for the group's approach to this four-part process, we do not seek to provide a detailed plan. We believe that drawing up such a plan would be done best by members of the group involved, after study and discussion of our book's more general recommendations. In fact, just making those decisions would be an excellent step in developing the kind of dialogue we'll be recommending. Still, if the group would prefer to have such a plan in hand, JustFaith Ministries provides a facilitator's guide to be used in conjunction with our book. But even when using a detailed plan or program, each group should feel free to adapt it to its own needs. Our intention is to help groups achieve independence from a particular procedure, while at the same time supplying every possible help for informed decision-making.

One study aid we do supply, however, is a set of discussion questions located at the end of each of the eight chapters. These questions have a double purpose: to reinforce the group's focus on the particular chapter's key themes as well as to challenge the group to apply these themes to their own growing sense of mission.

Model for Our Encounter:
The Meeting between Francis and the Sultan

In 1219,* near Damietta, Egypt, during a lull in the bloody fighting of the Fifth Crusade, Francis of Assisi somehow made his way safely through the lines of battle to the tent serving as headquarters of the enemy, Sultan Malik al-Kamil. His aim was to end the slaughter (and save the Sultan's soul) by converting him to the true faith, Christianity, or, failing that, to die as a martyr. Either outcome would have been glorious, to Francis's way of thinking.

The actual outcome was different, yet arguably no less glorious. Instead of converting the Sultan or of undergoing martyrdom, Francis found spiritual companionship with the man he assumed to be his mortal enemy, the dreaded Saracen Malik himself.

Francis's openness to the possibility of such companionship, even in an age of extreme hostility between Christianity and Islam, shouldn't surprise us. Francis had already made a practice of breaking down barriers. He approached all people, including lepers, as brothers and sisters. Francis saw no great accomplishment in this. Hadn't Christ himself done the same? And hadn't Christ told us to "love the enemy"? Hadn't Christ put that preaching into practice even when caught in the enemy's grip? Francis thought he was doing no more than Christ had asked him to do, and he hoped he was doing it in Christ's spirit of peace.

---

*All the dates in this book follow the Gregorian calendar.

What did Francis actually say to the Sultan? We don't know. No eyewitness account of their conversations exists. But clearly the two men did hold conversations, and friendly if challenging ones at that. They did not vilify each other's religions, that much we can assume. Yet we must also assume that they did not engage in "interfaith dialogue" in our modern understanding of the phrase. Within the limitations imposed upon them by the age in which they lived, they still managed to listen to each other and to find much to admire in what each other had to say about their respective faiths. There are hints that their response went even beyond admiration. There are hints that they allowed themselves to be influenced by what they heard. Francis, we know, was particularly impressed by the Muslim discipline of *salat* (daily prayer) and by Muslim devotion to the Ninety-Nine Beautiful Names of God. What he heard from the Sultan may have strengthened his own commitment to comparable Christian practices.

And the Sultan? Why did he not pounce on Francis and slay him on the spot when Francis embarked on his stated goal of converting him to Christianity? We can only guess at the reason. The Sultan, we know, was a peace loving man. He offered many overtures of peace to the papal legate, Bishop Pelagius, all of which were turned down. (Francis himself probably bore one of these offers to Pelagius on his return from the Sultan's camp.) The Sultan was also very familiar with Sufism, the inward, spiritual practice of Islam. He must have instantly recognized in Francis a kindred spirit. He must have seen that Francis's desire to convert him to Christianity was born of love, not of contempt. The Sultan must have seen too that when he urged upon Francis the great virtues of Prophet Muhammad, Francis listened with true interest and respect. Both must have recognized that their religious differences were transcended by a brotherhood of faith in the One God.

This, we can say, was a beautiful encounter. The two men acted beautifully in the midst of ugliness. But the beauty was God's before it was theirs. God's beauty called Francis and the Sultan out of enmity and warfare and drew them toward Himself, the source of peace and joy. The closer Francis and the Sultan drew to God, the more beautiful they became. They were transformed in the image of the source of peace and joy. Not all the accumulated ugliness of prejudice, not all the blood of battle could diminish this transformation. God's beauty, and the willingness of the two men to be the servants of that beauty, triumphed over the ugliness.

But the beauty they manifested in and through each other was not their private possession. The beauty was a sign of their commitment to the love of their fellow-creatures as much as it was a commitment to their love of God. Both men went forth from their tent of meeting strengthened in their calling to become servant-leaders. Both men are renowned to this day for the kindness and compassion of their behavior to the least fortunate. True, neither was able to bring the Crusades to an end or eliminate suffering from the world. But by the very fact of their meeting peacefully, as friends of God — though mortal enemies in human terms — they created new possibilities for Christian-Muslim relations, possibilities we Christians and Muslims have only begun to realize.

These possibilities have not been diminished by the bloody course of recent events. The smoke and misery of war did not deter Francis and the Sultan from dedicating themselves to works of peace. Surrounded by comparable ugliness, Christians and Muslims in our own time continue to be called by the God who is beautiful to be beautiful in his image, and to bring beauty out of ugliness in the world around us. We are called, just as Francis and the Sultan once were, to cross our contemporary lines of battle to meet each other on holy ground, where we see God's beauty all the more clearly by seeing it reflected in each other's faces. And where, strengthened by that vision, we go forth to build the world of the Kingdom, of *salaam*, of just relationships, that God has called us both to inhabit.

We will make sure, however, to invite St. Francis and the Sultan along with us on the journey marked out for us by this book. We will do that by recalling, at each stage of our way, how those two spiritual giants approached similar challenges in their own time. Our time is different, of course. But we can still learn much and draw confidence from their example. At the beginning of each of the chapters that follow, we'll be checking in with them in their tent at Damietta to see where their experience might be paralleling and illuminating our own.

Part 1

Building Confidence

Chapter 1

FINDING COMMON SYMBOLS

Retracing the Path of Francis and the Sultan: First Steps

As we said in our Introduction, St. Francis and Sultan Malik al-Kamil met in the Sultan's tent during a lull in the fighting of the Fifth Crusade in 1219 in Damietta, Egypt. We also suggested Francis's probable purposes in initiating this dangerous visit, unarmed and accompanied only by his companion Illuminato: to end the bloodshed of the Fifth Crusade by converting the Sultan to the true faith, Christianity, or, failing that, to die as a martyr. Yet despite the unknowns facing him, Francis must have felt his chances of survival were good. He had very likely heard and been encouraged by stories of Malik's humanity. These stories competed with tales of the Sultan's bloodthirstiness circulating in the Crusaders' encampment. Francis was brave, but he was no fool. He saw a chance to bring an end to the mutual carnage by means of the Sultan's conversion. He was willing to take that chance.

Some accounts insist that St. Francis and his companion, Illuminato, were roughed up by the Sultan's soldiers as they made their way through the battle lines to the Sultan's tent. But they did arrive safely, a fact attributable either to divine miracle or to the natural respect St. Francis inspired or to both. The energy and creativity of St. Francis's subsequent behavior suggests that he was little the worse for wear.

Since no record of the conversation of Francis and the Sultan at Damietta was kept, we can't say for sure how their meeting began. But judging by the positive and mutually transforming way it ended, we can guess that the two quickly found common ground with each other. How did they do that?

Their success couldn't have been accidental. Both, we know for certain, were prayerful men. Both would have prayed for guidance before their meeting. Francis's prayers would have been the more urgent. Even supposing that Francis was aware of Sultan Malik's reputation for seeking peaceful solutions to conflict, Francis had no assurance that the Sultan would be responsive to the kind of mission on which Francis came. How would the Sultan react to Francis's effort of evangelization? Would he feel insulted? Incensed? Or would the Holy Spirit find a way through Francis's agency to open the Sultan to the saving grace of Christ? With God's help, all things were possible.

Crucial for the direction their interview soon took, however, was Francis's evangelical manner. We'll look closely at his formation as a Christian in chapter 3 to understand the origin of this manner. For now, though, we can say that he never approached evangelization aggressively or self-righteously, thundering threats and denunciations right and left. Rather, he sought to embody the teachings of Christ rather than to insist on them. "Preach constantly," he is reputed to have said, then adding, "and sometimes in words." Accordingly, in approaching his interview with Sultan Malik, he would have wanted to present himself as the fairest possible model of his faith. And that meant finding a way to embody Christ's hospitality. What common symbols of his faith could he exchange with the Sultan to help him understand the depth of his commitment to serve God and God's creatures joyfully and faithfully?

Perhaps the words Francis used in greeting served part of this function. Before his death, on October 3, 1226, Francis recorded in his Testament that "the Lord revealed a greeting to me that we should say, 'May the Lord give you peace'" (*Test.* 23). This greeting, we're told, ruffled those of his own faith for whom Christianity had become a militant religion, one that provided the faithful with the determination to fight against enemies of all kinds: rebellious subjects, heretics, pagans, and, of course, Muslims. But the Sultan would very likely have heard the greeting differently. He might have reflected on its similarity to his own customary Muslim greeting, *As-salaam aleikum,* or Peace be with you. He might even have replied to his guest in the same words, despite the fact that normally *As-salaam aleikum* is addressed only by one Muslim to another.

The likelihood that he did so is increased if we try to imagine the effect Francis's simple brown habit would have had on the Sultan. Francis came before Sultan Malik dressed not as a man of war but as a monk. His appearance could well have recalled to the Sultan those verses of the Qur'an where Christian monks are held in the highest esteem.

> You will find that nearest in love to Muslim believers are those who say, "We are Christians" — because among them are priests (men who are devoted to learning) as well as monks (those who have fled from the world in fear), for these never puff themselves up. And when they listen to the message of the Qur'an handed down to the messenger Muhammad, you see their eyes overflowing with tears. For they perceive at once its truth, and they pray, "O Lord, we believe — write us down among the witnesses." (Sura al-Ma'idah 5:82–83)

The monks' fear is viewed positively in the Qur'an because it accords with the inner meaning of *islam:* a self-yielding to God that vigorously rejects all competing idolatrous claims and worldly motives. Proof of the monks' *islam* is their openness to God's voice. The voice penetrates their hearts. The tears that then fill their eyes express what Christians used to call *penthos,* compunction: sorrow for sin mixed with the hope of pardon. The genuineness of the monks' self-yielding response is the point of the Qur'anic passage. There is no further claim that they were thereby obliged to convert to Islam as a religion separate from Christianity.

But why assume that such a passage would have had a direct effect on Sultan Malik, softening his heart and causing him to override the natural antagonism he might have been expected to feel toward the infidel enemy, monk or not?

After we learn more about Sultan Malik in chapter 4, we'll be in a better position to answer that question. But one point about Sultan Malik can be advanced right now: Disposing Sultan Malik in Francis's favor was the Sultan's awareness of the similarity between Christian monks and Sufis, Islam's own spiritual athletes and ascetics. Sultan Malik's attraction to and respect for Sufis are well attested. The brown habit of Francis might have recalled that attraction. It could well have provided the key common symbol smoothing the way for their encounter.

The name *sufi* means "wool," referring to the plain coarse gowns worn by Sufi students and masters. Sufis do not represent a separate sect of Islam. Rather, they embody the inward, meditative impulse that is a key dimension of Islam itself, a dimension that over the centuries has sought to balance Islam's extroverted, legalistic aspect. The Qur'an itself, with its emphasis on the *batin* and the *zohir*, the hidden and the overt dimensions of faith, enforces a duality within the believer. The inner work of self-yielding to God must be complemented by the outer work of service to others. Sufis are those who in time came to maintain schools continuing and augmenting the teachings and spiritual practices of previous spiritual masters.

One such teacher was Sultan Malik's own religious adviser, Fakhr al-Farisi, himself a follower of the great Persian mystic, Mansur al-Hallaj. Al-Hallaj so greatly identified himself with Jesus that he submitted to crucifixion in Baghdad in 922 rather than recant his ecstatic witness that "I am the truth." Indeed, Sufis were known for their idealization of Jesus as an ascetic saint, as we shall see when we discuss Muslim images of Jesus in chapter 3.

Common symbols, like the greeting they might have used with each other and especially the habit Francis wore, helped persuade the Sultan to receive Francis as a brother in faith. Other influences would have persuaded the Sultan as well, notably the influence of family tradition and teaching in favor of resolving conflicts peacefully (topics we'll discuss in chapter 4). The exchange of symbols enabled the two men to take the first step, that of building mutual trust, so that eventually the task of bringing peace to their war-torn world could go forward. Part of that subsequent work would involve confronting Christianity's and Islam's great and in some instances irreconcilable differences. But that confrontation could most profitably be handled later in their visit, once the initial bonds of friendship had been established.

Taking Our Own First Steps

Like Francis and the Sultan, Christians and Muslims gathering to build community in solidarity with each other and with the world's afflicted cannot avoid the all-important first steps of building confidence. They need to build confidence in many areas: confidence not only in themselves and in each other, but also in the value of their common goal — as well as in the practicality of the methods available for reaching it. Building this multifaceted confidence is an ongoing project. Each further step along the way right through to the end requires a constant deepening of relationships and self-understanding.

But the initial meeting of today's Muslim-Christian groups presents a particular challenge, just as it did for Francis and the Sultan. This challenge involves tracing commonalties between the two religions, commonalties of creed, symbol, and practice that are most easily and joyfully understood and accepted by both faiths. Without an appreciation of such commonalties, dialogue cannot begin. With them, groups can begin the process of discovering and developing positive relationships. Dealing with differences can be left for later.

Clearly, fruitful interfaith dialogue requires patience. Each stage has its own strengths and limitations. Participants have to resist the temptation to rush ahead (to engage right away in social justice projects, for example) until they have thoughtfully and prayerfully sorted through what binds them together — and what separates them. Interfaith dialogue has a dynamic that is thoroughly human in the best sense, meaning that it incorporates the whole person, body, soul, and spirit, in its development. Intellectual understanding isn't enough. The emotions and the imagination must be engaged as well. And lasting friendships, as we all know, take time to develop.

Commonalties of Creeds

Before we look at specific symbols and practices Islam and Christianity share, we need to compare the religious creeds and structures of which those symbols and practices are an expression. We'll start by laying out in schematic form the creed, first of one religion (Islam), then of the other (Christianity). We'll compare the creeds afterward, emphasizing commonalties and reserving for chapter 2 an assessment of differences. Then we'll compare the religious structures to which Islam's and Christianity's creeds lead the believer. Once the commonalties of creeds and structures are firmly in place, we'll look at the symbols and practices that emerge from those structures but that also, because of the flexibility of symbols, bridge the two religions, revealing their deeper unity.

The Creed of Islam

Islam's creed, compared to Christianity's, is extremely brief. It is expressed in a single statement containing two affirmations: "There is no god but God and Muhammad is his messenger." The first affirmation asserts the utter unicity of God; the second identifies a particular historical person, Muhammad, as the bearer of that One God's message to humankind. Or put another way, the first affirmation defines the nature of the source of all that exists, while the second validates the means by which this source has chosen to communicate with its human creation. Both affirmations have their origins in the Qur'an itself; the first affirmation ("There is no god but God") is a direct quotation, frequently repeated throughout the Qur'anic text. The second ("Muhammad is his messenger") is a paraphrase of Qur'anic verses similar to it.

Islam's creed dates from the religion's earliest days, that is, from some time after 610, when the Prophet Muhammad first began receiving the revelations that came to be known as the Qur'an. This creed has never been changed or modified. Known as the *shahadah,* or "witness," in Arabic, this creed forms the first of Islam's Pillars. (More about the Pillars shortly.) The *shahadah* is the public affirmation of the individual's desire to embrace the Muslim faith. It is said initially within a setting of worship to confirm the individual's place within the Muslim *umma,* or community. But as a remembrance of that commitment the *shahadah* continues to be recited throughout the believer's life. The *shahadah* forms part of the *adhan,* or call to daily prayers, intoned by the *mu'adhdhan,* or caller, but repeated silently by the members of the gathering community. In this way not only their commitment but the basic content of their faith are constantly brought to Muslims' attention.

The Creed of Christianity

One of Christianity's earliest creeds, and one that is still widely used by a variety of Christian denominations, is the Apostles' Creed. The Creed's name comes from the legend that each of the twelve original followers (Apostles) of Jesus dictated one of its twelve articles under the inspiration of the Holy Spirit at the celebration of Pentecost, a Jewish feast that fell fifty days after Jesus' resurrection. While scholars dispute this account, they are in general agreement that the Apostles' Creed, or an earlier version of it, dates back at least to the second century.

Following is the text of the Apostles' Creed in the ecumenical version of the English Language Liturgical Consultation (ELLC):

> I believe in God, the Father almighty, creator of heaven and
> earth.
> I believe in Jesus Christ, God's only Son, our Lord,
> who was conceived by the Holy Spirit, born of the Virgin
> Mary,

suffered under Pontius Pilate, was crucified, died, and was
    buried;
he descended into hell. On the third day he rose again;
he ascended into heaven, he is seated at the right hand of
    the Father,
and he will come to judge the living and the dead.
I believe in the Holy Spirit,
the holy catholic Church,
the communion of saints,
the forgiveness of sins,
the resurrection of the body,
and the life everlasting. Amen.

The Apostles' Creed is obviously much longer than the Muslim *shahadah*. And it certainly looks more complex. Yet it actually exhibits the same structure: an affirmation of the One God followed by the identification of a particular historical individual, in this case Jesus, as the bearer of that One God's message to humankind. Yet in Christian belief, that historical individual is also God, whereas for Muslims Jesus is simply and strictly human, a man and a prophet, like Muhammad himself. And the Holy Spirit, in Christian belief, is God as well. The Holy Spirit is believed by Christians to be the third person of the Trinity. In function the Holy Spirit binds the Father and the Son together in love and brings faithful humanity into the divine life.

Muslims cannot, of course, accept such an understanding of God as Three in One. We will consider this difference more closely in the following chapter. For now, though, we note that, as in the *shahadah,* the first affirmation ("I believe in God") of the Apostles' Creed defines the nature of the source of all that exists, while the second ("I believe in Jesus Christ. . . . I believe in the Holy Spirit") validates the means by which this source has chosen to communicate with its human creation. (Affirmations of belief in the church, the forgiveness of sins, etc., follow from the first two affirmations.) While the Creed's language is not directly biblical, its phrases can all be traced back to words or concepts used in the New Testament.

In use as well the Apostles' Creed plays a role similar to that played by the *shahadah*. The Creed, in question-and-answer form, has an important function at a comparable once-in-a-lifetime event, at the individual's baptism. By assenting to its provisions the candidate confirms his or her desire to become a member of the Christian community. And as a remembrance of that commitment the Apostles' Creed continues to be recited at Sunday worship in many denominations. As the *shahadah* does for Muslims, the Creed brings both the memory of their commitment and the basic content of their faith constantly to Christians' attention.

The human faculties to which both the *shahadah* and the Creed appeal are not only the will and the intellect, however. They call forth the full range of human faculties: the will and intellect for sure, but also the imagination, all under the guidance of faith.

The *shahadah* and the Creed seek to arouse the fullest human response to the revelation God continues to offer humankind through God's word, primarily in Islam through the word of the Qur'an, primarily in Christianity through the Word who is Jesus Christ. (In chapter 2 we'll lay out some ways these two "words" are both alike and utterly different.) Both the Creed and the *shahadah* seek to enlist the whole person in service to God.

Commonalties of Structure

Islam's Structure

Because of their role in initiating people into their respective faiths, the *shahadah* and the Creed act like doorways into a greater architecture. Through them, the new believer enters a vast domain supported by three interlocking and interpenetrating elements: practice, belief, and spirituality, roughly corresponding to the faculties of body, mind (including will, intellect, and imagination), and spirit.

Because of its brevity, the *shahadah* does not reveal the full extent of this architecture. We do see the architecture revealed, however, in the Jibril Hadith (a *hadith* is an authenticated account of the Prophet Muhammad's sayings and actions). In the Jibril Hadith the Prophet is approached by a mysterious white-haired figure identified with the angel Jibril (Gabriel). The stranger asks the Prophet to name the fundamentals of the religion that God is revealing to and through him. The Prophet promptly, and to the stranger's satisfaction, names three fundamentals in order of their relation to the outer and inner dimensions of worship mentioned above in our discussion of Sufism:

> ('Umar, a Companion of the Prophet, reported:) One day while we were sitting with the Messenger of God (Allah), may God's peace and blessing be upon him, there appeared a man with very white clothing and very black hair; no sign of travel could be seen on him and none of us knew him. He sat next to the Prophet so that their knees were touching and placed his hands on his thighs. He said, "O Muhammad, tell me about *islam*." The Messenger of God said, "*Islam* is to testify that there is none worthy of worship but God and that Muhammad is the Messenger of God, to establish prayers, to pay the *zakat,* to fast the month of Ramadan, and to make pilgrimage to the House (the Ka'ba in Mecca) if you have the means to do so." (The man) said, "You have spoken truthfully." We were amazed that he had asked a question and (the Prophet) had spoken truthfully. (The man) said, "Tell me about *iman* (faith)." (The Prophet) said, "It is to believe in God, His angels, His scriptures, His messengers, the Last Day, and to believe in *qadr* (divine decree), both the good and the evil of it." He said, "You have spoken truthfully." Then he said, "Then tell me about *ihsan* (excellence)." (The Prophet) answered, "It is to worship God as if you see Him, and even though you do not see Him, you know that He sees you. . . . " In the end [the Prophet] said, "That was Jibril (Gabriel) who came to teach you your *din* (way of worship)."[1]

One point to establish at the outset is that the word "Allah" is simply the name for God in the Arabic language. "Allah" does not refer to a God separate from the one Jews and Christians worship, but to the same God, despite the fact that Judaism, Christianity, and Islam understand God's nature differently.

The second point to establish about the Jibril Hadith is that in it the word *islam* is used in what for us today seems a restricted sense. For the last two hundred years or so "Islam" has been used as a general term to refer to the religion of Muslims. But the word *islam* simply means "self-surrender," and often that is its meaning within the Qur'an itself. *Islam* refers to the desired allegiance all believers in the One God owe him: complete self-surrender. *Muslim*, a related word, accordingly means "he who has surrendered himself to God." Christians are echoing the belief expressed in *islam* when they ask, in the Lord's Prayer, "thy will be done."

As used in the Jibril Hadith, however, *islam* refers neither to self-surrender in the generic sense nor to a particular religion as distinct from other religions. It refers instead to the external practices of the community of believers that had formed around the revelations handed down to the Prophet Muhammad. Accordingly, the Prophet Muhammad names *islam* as the first fundamental of the community's way of worship, a fundamental established through faithful observance of what came to be called the Five Pillars: (1) public witness to the oneness of God and to Muhammad's prophetic calling (the *shahadah*); (2) daily prayer; (3) almsgiving (*zakat*) and (4) fasting, especially during the holy month of Ramadan; and (5) pilgrimage to Mecca undertaken once in one's life if one is financially and physically able.

As the second fundamental the Prophet names *iman*, or belief, or, even better, trust. *Iman* consists of six tenets: (1) belief in the One God; (2) belief in the angels as his servants and messengers; (3) belief in the Day of Judgment; (4) belief in the prophets (including Jesus); (5) belief in the prophets' basic message, summed up in the two commandments familiar both to Jews and Christians, that we are to love and serve God and God alone and that we are to care for God's creation; and (6) belief in God's provision of good and evil as humankind's fundamental choice determining the judgment they will receive on the Last Day.

And as the third fundamental the Prophet names *ihsan,* or beauty, here meaning the goal of spiritual virtue, or transparency of heart, as a result of which we are to live always in the most intimate possible awareness of God's presence. This awareness can be achieved only through an *islam* (in the sense of self-surrender) that incorporates not only external behavior but the most prayerful spiritual discipline, a discipline that can overcome, with Allah's grace, the many deceits of ego that constantly beset us through the whispering of Shaitan (Satan).

This three-part structure of *islam, iman,* and *ihsan* constitutes the structure of the religion we now call by the one name, Islam. One consequence of the expansion of this relatively recent use of the word *islam,* however, is that the entire religion can seem reduced to its external practices only. That is why Islam has sometimes been characterized as a religion of "orthopraxy" ("right behavior") rather than of "orthodoxy" ("right belief"). It has also been characterized as a religion of "works" rather than of "faith." Such a characterization is justified only in the sense that "works" or practices were from the beginning a critical measure defining the Muslim community. This is because of the chaotic social context into which the revelations to Muhammad first came. Arabia in the early seventh century. was a congeries of polytheistic nomadic tribes without any conception of a common good or of universally binding moral behavior. A key element of the Qur'anic revelations has to do with the stabilization of what was at the time (and continually tended to revert to) a lawless world of ongoing tribal warfare.

But the characterization misses altogether the complexity of the structure sketched in the Jibril Hadith. "Works" (*islam*) are meaningless without faith (*iman*) — as well as without spirituality (*ihsan*). Normatively, all three elements are of equal importance and function best when practiced together. Depending on their personal gifts or upon historical or political factors Muslims may seem to accentuate one element over another. Practical people and jurists will tend to emphasize the importance of *islam.* Scholars will tend to emphasize *iman.* For Sufis, *ihsan* is the goal. But all well-educated Muslims recognize the ultimate importance of integrating the three elements. They know that to detach one element from the others is to distort their religion. For example, detaching *ihsan* (spirituality) from *iman* (belief) and *islam* (practices) results in dangerously vague self-absorption, without grounding either in principle or in communal practice. Likewise, detaching *islam* (practices) from *iman* (belief) and *ihsan* (spirituality) results in literal-minded fixation on external observance, uninformed by reason and closed to the spirit. And *iman* (belief) without *islam* (practices) and *ihsan* (spirituality) shrinks from a trusting assent to God's promises to dry cognitive content. The integrative behavior enjoined on all Muslims is exemplified in the life of Rumi, the world-renowned poet, who was a Muslim scholar and jurist as well as one of the greatest of Sufis.

Christianity's Structure

Unlike the *shahadah,* the Apostles' Creed does reveal the religion's structure. Christianity's structure is different from Islam's, just as we'd expect, though the same or similar elements are present.

The Jibril Hadith provides a good lens for highlighting what those similar elements are. Take for example the Jibril Hadith's understanding of *islam,* of external practices. The Creed's key roles both in the rite of baptism and in Sunday celebrations figure as Christian versions of *islam,* as activities that define and govern the common life and behavior of those who adhere to the Christian faith. The content of the Creed figures as Christianity's *iman,* that is, those articles of belief that are to be understood not only intellectually but are also to be assented to as sure signs of what God has done and will do for humankind. Several of those articles echo those found in the *iman* of Islam: belief in the One God; belief in angels (though some Christian denominations emphasize this belief more than others); belief in the Day of Judgment (in fact, according to Qur'an verse 4:159, Jesus will appear on that Day, not as judge of humankind, however, but as witness); belief in the basic message of the Prophets; and belief in God's providing humankind with a fundamental choice between good and evil. Other articles listed in the Creed but not under *iman* in the Jibril Hadith would also be accepted by Islam: belief in God's forgiveness (one of Allah's "Beautiful Names" is *ar-rahim*, the Most Merciful); belief in the resurrection of the dead; and belief in everlasting life. Finally, the Creed shares with Islam an emphasis on the universality of its truths (catholicity) and on the importance of community (communion).

What the lens of the Jibril Hadith also reveals, however, is a seeming imbalance in Christianity as revealed through the Apostles' Creed. Just as Islam can (unfairly) be reduced to a religion of "works" (of *islam* in the restricted sense), Christianity can, equally unfairly, be reduced to a religion of "belief," in the sense of *iman*, since *iman* is all that the Creed seems to focus on. The reduction can be justified only in the sense that "belief" was from the beginning a critical measure for the Christianity community, just as we saw above that "works" was a critical measure for defining the Muslim community. Christianity did not emerge in a lawless polytheistic context, as Islam did, but as a grassroots reform movement within a monotheistic religion, Judaism, which had become hostage to the occupying imperial power of Rome. The movement was utterly transformed, however, by an event that came as a shock and surprise even to those who knew and loved Jesus best: the revelation of his identity as God's Son through his resurrection from the dead. How and in what terms to articulate their understanding of this revelation became, and remains, a besetting challenge to Christians.

Yet as with Islam, to reduce Christianity to only one of its facets is to miss altogether the complexity of its structure. Here again the Jibril Hadith is helpful, for if we look more closely at the Apostles' Creed through it, we'll find that all the human faculties are engaged, not just will and intellect (the faculties associated with *islam* and *iman*). *Ihsan* (spirituality) is also revealed and engaged. And we'll find as well that these various faculties are meant to function together, just as they are in Islam.

The key to grasping this fullness is to realize that the Creed's listing of the "career" of Jesus Christ, beginning with His descent into human flesh at conception; to his suffering, crucifixion, death, and burial; to his further descent into hell; to his rising on the third day; and to his ascent to heaven — that this listing is far more than a catalogue of events whose veracity Christians are obliged to accept. This listing describes the Christian life itself. For at baptism Christians believe they die and rise again into Christ's own life through the power of the Holy Spirit. Christians, in Paul the Apostle's phrase, are called to "put on Christ." When they do so (in baptism), Christ now lives in them. Or to describe their baptismal transformation in Muslim terms, Christians enter at baptism into *ihsan:* into a condition of utter transparency to God's invitation to participate in the divine life as adopted sons and daughters. The transformation is not completed during one's lifetime, however. But Christians believe in the power of God's grace to bring them to fullness of life in the world to come. They believe that this grace is mediated through the Holy Spirit, ever-active in the lives of Christians to enable them to break free from the chains of all forms of sinfulness. Other elements of their religion, namely, practices and beliefs, strengthen Christian believers and open them to the Holy Spirit's assistance on their journey toward the intimacy with God promised them.

Approaching Symbols

Symbols play a key role in both Islam and Christianity. Indeed symbols are among the main tools God uses to communicate God's desires to humankind. In the Qur'an's Sura an-Nur 24:35, for example, we hear: "God speaks to humankind in symbols." In the Christian Gospels Jesus' preferred manner of instruction is through parables, which are symbols that take the form of stories.

Symbols aren't merely things that stand for other things, however. Symbols are ways of conveying spiritual realities in concrete terms. The concreteness of expression calls forth not just the senses but the imagination and the intellect too. Symbols engage the fullest human response to a message God desires to convey to us.

In general, however, Christians weigh symbols more heavily than Muslims do. For Christians, sacraments are "effective symbols." Effective symbols are physical gestures or things that do far more than represent a spiritual reality. Effective symbols, through God's gracious, merciful response to people's prayers, actually become what they signify. So the water of baptism does more than bathe the one being baptized. The water becomes the vehicle of death to sin and resurrection to life in Jesus Christ. Sacraments are the means by which Christ becomes present in the believer.

Christians who belong to liturgical churches (among whom are Catholics, Episcopalians, Lutherans, and Eastern Orthodox) accept, besides baptism, up to six other sacraments: confirmation, Eucharist, marriage, confession, anointing of the sick, and ordination, depending on the denomination. But all Christians insist on God's continuing transformation of common elements — water, at least — into the site of the Holy Spirit's direct action. Muslims maintain a much stricter sense of God's separation from the matter God is constantly bringing into being.

As a result of these fundamental differences of belief, Christians and Muslims have to be very careful about the way they talk about their shared symbols. Muslims need to be aware that Christians might be investing a particular symbol with meanings that Muslims simply cannot embrace. Christians need to be aware that Muslims are almost certainly *not* investing a particular symbol with those meanings. Muslims can't let themselves become scandalized by the apparent "overload" of Christian symbolic investment. Christians can't let themselves become scandalized by Muslim symbolic "undervaluation." Each group, recognizing its differences of belief, must respect those differences and be content with the meanings they do share.

As Muslims and Christians become more comfortable with each other, they can return to a discussion of symbols with real freedom and interest. Everyone benefits from this kind of relaxed but focused exchange. Christians may find themselves forced to recognize that their own understanding of sacraments needs a lot of sharpening, under pressure from sincerely interested questions from their Muslim friends. Muslims may have to face a similar humbling moment when sincerely asked by their Christian friends how a transcendent God can also be "closer than one's jugular vein" (see Sura Qaf 50:16). Neither group would be trying to put the other on the spot. The desire of each to understand the Other better would have the healthy result of making both parties more aware of the mystery of God's love and care for them.

Commonalties of Symbols

Now that we've established a sense of the commonalties of creed and structure that Islam and Christianity share, we can look at a few of the symbols that emerge from those creeds and structures as their most vivid and engaging signs or representations. We'll look at the symbols that Islam and Christianity have in common, weighing both the meanings that Islam and Christianity don't share and the meanings they do.

Meal — The Differences

First, the differences. For Christians, the Meal is a symbol of their communion with Jesus Christ. The model for the Meal is the Last Supper, which Jesus held with his twelve apostles prior to his crucifixion, an event described in great detail in each of the four Christian Gospels. As a result of the Reformation most Protestant churches tend to treat the Meal as a memorial of Jesus' self-sacrificing desire to share his life with his followers. The liturgical churches, however, preserve the earlier understanding of the Meal as a sharing of Christ's very body and blood. The Meal embodies, for these churches, a direct divine-human transaction enabled by God through the Holy Spirit. The Meal celebrates God's merciful desire to allow his creatures to share through their communion with him and with each other in God's divine life.

For Muslims, the Meal is celebratory also, but in a much more restricted sense. Especially in the two great feasts or *Eids* that conclude the month of Ramadan and the *hajj* respectively, the Meal enables Muslims to rejoice in their present unity following from their individual self-surrender to God, a self-surrender enabled (but not forced) by God's gracious *fadl,* favor. Muslims rejoice too in the future *salaam* of the great banquet of resurrected and perfected souls in the Garden. But the Meal never becomes the means of divine-human sharing.

Meal — The Commonalties

In the Meal, Christians and Muslims can acknowledge God's desire that by eating together they behave as people anticipating the joy of their unanimity as members of the one family of God. (Christians will recall Paul's rebuke of the Corinthians for relegating their poorer members to a lower table, in 1 Corinthians 11:17–34.) Nothing prevents Christians and Muslims from inventing ways of speaking of their meals together as symbolizing the fullness of human sharing for which they all long.

Light — The Differences

For Muslims, light is a transcendent attribute of the One God, best exemplified in the Qur'an's "Light Verse," in Sura an-Nur 24:35. (Many Muslims believe this to be the most beautiful verse in the Qur'an.):

> God is the light of heaven and earth.
> The parable of his light is like a niche
> in which there is a lamp,
> and the lamp is in a glass,
> and the glass is like a radiant star
> lit by the oil of a blessed olive tree
> neither of the west nor of the east;
> yet it is as if this oil itself would shine
> though no fire touch it.
> Light upon light!
> God guides to God's light
> the one God wills to guide,
> and the one who wills to be guided.

> God speaks to humankind in symbols,
> for God is beyond all measure
> in God's knowledge of created things.

But for Christians, the divine light is not an attribute of God. The Light is God Himself, in Christ, as proclaimed in John's Gospel, especially 1:1–5. (Many Christians believe these verses to be the most beautiful in the New Testament.):

> In the beginning was the Word, and the Word was with God, and the Word was God. He was in the beginning with God. All things came into being through him, and without him not one thing came into being. What has come into being in him was life, and the life was the light of all people. The light shines in the darkness, and the darkness did not overcome it.

This difference is not trivial. It goes right to the heart of what divides Muslims and Christians in their understanding of God. In chapter 2, we'll address this difference in the context of asking whether and how Christians and Muslims can pray together.

Light — The Commonalties

For both religions, light symbolizes God's beauty and glory, the source and stimulus of human enlightenment and spiritual flourishing. Muslims and Christians can invoke the symbol of light to honor God's beauty without feeling they are betraying their own particular beliefs about precisely what light signifies.

Water — The Differences

For Muslims, water is an agent of purification, used before each of the five daily prayers (the second Pillar of Islam, known as *salat*) in a cleansing ritual called *wudu*. *Wudu* reminds Muslims that in addressing God they must move from the profane world to the world set apart for human communication with the divine. For Christians, water symbolizes the transforming interaction of the risen Christ with the believer as he or she dies to sin and is reborn in baptism. And Christ continues to give believers the water of eternal life, as he did long ago to the Samaritan woman (see John 4:4–33). He also enables us to become the servants of others as he once did when he washed the disciples' feet in John 13:1–17.

Water — The Commonalties

Again, water contains overlapping meanings that Christians and Muslims can make good use of. Cleansing would be chief among these, reflecting the emphasis both faiths place on the goal of spiritual purity or singleness of heart, or *ihsan,* in Muslim terminology.

Path — The Differences

Yes, there are differences. Islam's history is grounded in particular examples of paths and pilgrimage, especially in the Prophet Muhammad's emigration from Mecca to Medina in 622 and in his triumphant return in 630. Islam's present is to a great extent shaped by one of the Pillars of Islam, the *hajj,* the yearly pilgrimage on the part of the entire worldwide community of Muslims to the physical center of worship, at the Ka'bah at Mecca. Words for path abound in Islam, including *sabil, surat, tariq,* and *shari'a.* Each of these has a particular application to the guidance God gives believers as they hasten toward their goal.

Perhaps Muslims have remained more faithful to the concept of the path than Christians have. Yet the symbolic value of path is still strong among Christians. Jesus identified himself as both the "way" and the goal (the "life") in John 14:4–6. The earliest name of those who followed the risen Christ wasn't "Christians." They called themselves "people of the Way" in Acts 19:23. During his lifetime Jesus often said to his followers, "Follow me." And Christians often speak of their great liturgical seasons as journeys: the journeys of Advent and of Lent, for example. The practice of observing the "Stations" or Way of the Cross is another example of the Christian experience as a journey, as a following of Jesus. Some Christians still observe the practice of pilgrimage when they take trips to the Holy Land of Israel or to the shrine of St. James in Compostela, Spain.

Path — The Commonalties

This is perhaps the "safest" of the common symbols. The overlapping here is extensive.

Christianity and Islam are religions of pilgrimage. For both, human life in this world is a community's journey through time to the timelessness of the world to come, where what is incomplete or broken in believers individually and as a community will be healed and fulfilled. The path of this journey is well marked. Through revelation and through the example of his saints and prophets God lays out this path toward the goal of *salaam* (fullness, fruition) and of the Kingdom. God stands in judgment on our progress, but God is merciful to us when we stumble. God is ever-present to our need and distress. Falling, we have but to cry out to feel ourselves lifted up and strengthened and set moving forward again.

There are rich resources here for celebrating this very effort on which Christians and Muslims are embarked as a journey along a path. Christians and Muslims can do this without stressing meanings that would state or imply that they are walking every step of that path together. We might think of Christianity and Islam as parallel paths that nevertheless converge in order to promote the common good. One of the verses of the Qur'an's Sura al-Ma'idah 5:49 gives us warrant. Speaking to the People of the Message (that is, not only to Muslims, but to Jews and Christians as well), God says, "Strive together as in a race in doing works of justice." It would be hard to imagine a race being run on wholly different tracks! No, Muslims and Christians find themselves on the same path, though in different lanes. They are striving to best each other too, not in works of violence, but (as their brother and sister Jews say) in those of *tikkun olam,* healing the world. This is a race in which there can be no loser, and in which the path leads to the same Light.

Discussion Questions

1. Francis received in a revelation a special greeting: "May the Lord give you peace." Why did this greeting upset some of the Christians of his time? What is the connection between this revelation and the only other one Francis said he received, that he "should live according to the Pattern of the Holy Gospel" (*Test.* 14)?

2. Why is the Sufi tradition in Islam a possible bridge between the Sultan and Francis? Are the Sufis still a link for Christians and Muslims?

3. How would you summarize the similarities and the differences between the Apostles' Creed and the Muslim *shahadah*?

4. Why has Islam been characterized as a religion of "works" (orthopraxis) rather than a religion of "faith" (orthodoxy)?

5. Muslims and Christians see religious symbols in distinctive ways. Explain the differences. Use one of the symbols discussed in this chapter as a specific example of the differences and the commonalties.

Chapter 2

DEVELOPING
COMMON PRAYERS

Retracing the Path of Francis and the Sultan:
Praying to God Together

In chapter 1 we imagined St. Francis and the Sultan's first steps in building mutual trust. Their success in taking these steps depended on their readiness to respect each other's cultural assumptions and practices, especially those involving hospitality. But success depended even more on their willingness to tolerate each other's religious differences. Astonishingly — for suspicion and hostility between Muslims and Christians were the order of the day — the two men proved to be disposed not simply to tolerate but even to be open to each other's religious differences. We'll talk in chapters 3 and 4 about how the personal histories prior to their encounter at Damietta disposed both Francis and the Sultan to such openness. And in chapter 7 we'll describe the actions and behaviors their openness made possible during the several days they spent together.

What were the exact steps in this process of trust-building? Lacking a reliable eyewitness account of their meeting, we can't know for sure. But in view of the meeting's outcome, and taking into account what we know about each man's character and religious commitment, we can assume, as we did in chapter 1, that they moved quickly to a tentative exploration of their common religious vocabulary, that is, of their common religious symbols. Perhaps, as we suggested, the similarity between their greetings of peace together with their shared attraction to spiritual simplicity (the "Sufi" habit of Francis) gave them confidence to explore those symbols.

But religious symbols don't exist for themselves. Symbols are, at a minimum, the currency for the way we imagine our relationship to God in prayer (while at a maximum, for the majority of Christians, symbols are sacraments enabling divine-human exchange). So very soon St. Francis and the Sultan must have been testing whether and how symbols might serve as currency not only for their dialogue with each other, but for their dialogue with God in prayer. We can imagine a series of questions occurring to both of them, beginning with: Could they pray to God together? And if the answer seemed to be "Yes," then we can imagine them asking, What would "praying together" mean? Would it mean praying their own respective Christian and Muslim prayers side-by-side — separately, but respectful of each other's manner of worship? Or could it possibly mean praying to God in common, in one voice?

Much in their respective traditions would have quickly led them both to answer each of these questions with a resounding "*no.*" Even if St. Francis had not been aware of St. John Chrysostom's seventh-century polemic against Islam as a Christian heresy, he would have inherited John's negative assessment. Francis's compatriot Dante certainly did so, when, around 1300, some six or seven decades after the death of Francis, while writing the *Inferno,* he placed Muhammad deep in hell as chief of the Sowers of Discord.

For his part, the Sultan would have honored Jesus as a great prophet; the Sultan's Holy Book, the Qur'an, would have enjoined on him that much. But it would also have taught him to regard any worship of this great prophet as God as idolatry. If we add to such deep theological differences the ongoing holy war between Christians and Muslims inaugurated by Pope Urban II's calling of the First Crusade in 1095, then we can easily see how Francis and the Sultan's hope of praying to God together in any shape or form could have been a non-starter.

And so it would have been a non-starter if Francis and the Sultan had been ordinary men, typical products of their time and place. But they were not typical. Both believed that their religions enjoined peace with all God's creatures, even or even especially with their enemies. For if there really were only One God, as both affirmed, then "enemy" was merely a human category. The One God had made them all.

We have warrant for believing that they at least prayed together side by side and that each was respectfully attentive to the other's prayers. Whether they could have prayed in one voice is doubtful, given the exclusivist claims of their religions during this historical period. It is not impossible, however. At a minimum they must have come to understand that their prayers were directed to the same God and that this God listened to both men as they each prayed for peace, between themselves and between their co-religionists.

Can Christians and Muslims Pray in One Voice Today?

If praying side by side was even remotely an option for St. Francis and the Sultan in 1219, it is certainly an option for Christians and Muslims today, and a very desirable one.

Praying in one voice is more possible than it was in the time of Francis and the Sultan, but while desirable as well, it is not a practice to rush into without a lot of thought and discussion beforehand.

But why not? Why *can't* Muslims and Christians simply and without further ado pray in one voice to the One God in whom both believe? Yes, Muslims and Christians have differences in their beliefs about Jesus, but why should those particular differences become stumbling blocks in the path of their common mission to help bring God's *salaam* into our broken, needy world? Prayers of the proper type aren't hard to construct. All Muslims and Christians have to do is address them to God the Creator, omitting all reference to Jesus. That way, Muslims and Christians affirm the core beliefs they hold in common — in monotheism and in God as the merciful creator of all that is — without introducing beliefs where they are at odds, such as over Jesus' divinity.

And consider another advantage of simply leaving Jesus out of all prayers. Doesn't putting him *in* turn Jesus once again into a "scandal," literally a "stumbling block"? The chilling thought is that in just such a way, as "scandal," Jesus was treated during his lifetime by fellow Jews who could not accept his prophetic power (see Matthew 11:6, 13:57; Mark 6:3; Luke 7:23); and also after his death by Jews as well as Gentiles who could not accept his resurrection (see 1 Corinthians 1:23, 3:19; Romans 9:33; 1 Peter 2:8). Why force Muslims to seem to replay such negative roles? Is that fair to Muslims? How does putting them on the spot in this way advance the goal of encouraging interfaith cooperation?

There will be some Muslims and Christians who will nod in agreement with arguments like these. But there will be others, Christians and Muslims alike, who will find them objectionable.

The objection on the Christians' part will be that Jesus' identity can't be bracketed so easily or at all. For them, belief in Jesus' identity as God can never be a negotiable item, a minor element of faith that can be ignored or shelved for the sake of a "higher" purpose.

Muslims will object on different grounds. These Muslims will say: "How can a sincere Christian *not* pray to or through Christ? What does being a Christian mean if it doesn't mean *that*?" They would prefer to associate with Christians who are clear and forthright about their beliefs, even where those beliefs contradict the Muslims' own. In that case, however, praying together in one voice is out of the question. Their Christian counterparts would agree. And together they might add: "Is that a bad thing? Why, for that matter, is praying together in one voice important at all? Can't we Muslims and Christians be content with praying in our own distinctive ways, especially if we're praying for peace? Surely God hears our two prayers impartially. Why assume that praying in one voice would win greater divine favor?"

So here we have responses at two extremes to the question above, Can Christians and Muslims pray in one voice today? One voice says yes, the other no. But if the extremes can't in some way be reconciled, then the question dissolves into a matter of group temperament and personal preference. Easygoing natures will find praying together in one voice more acceptable than those with a stricter outlook.

It is very possible, however, that Muslims and Christians will lose more than they think they will gain by allowing the question to disappear in this way. What will be lost is the creative tension of searching together for God's light along what will certainly at times be a difficult path. Immediately initiating prayer in one voice collapses the tension right from the start. Categorically resisting it risks turning beliefs into suits of armor through which understanding of the other religion can never penetrate. The result, for Muslims and Christians embracing either extreme, is stagnation within the very area of thought and feeling that needs to be fertilized if the projects for the common good that are to issue from their gatherings are to bear fruit. Whether by leaping into praying with one voice or by digging in their heels against it, Muslims and Christians lose the chance to develop real understanding of what each other actually means by the words they're using in prayer, particularly those words — like "God" — which they share in common but which reveal distinctly different understandings.

It's true that persisting in a search for an understanding of God that transcends those differences doesn't take a neat and tidy shape. Muslims and Christians will need a great supply of the patience that both of their religions extol as one of the greatest virtues. But if they persist in their mutual pursuit, they will open themselves to unexpected and enriching insights not only about the religion of the Other, but about their "own" religion as well.

Accordingly, the path along which Muslims and Christians walk to engage the possibility of praying in one voice may be more important than whether they arrive at the prayer itself. In this chapter, we provide guidelines to help Muslims and Christians follow that path. The goal of praying in one voice lies before them. But the journey itself is a form of prayer, a way of thanking God together. Whether any particular group of Muslims and Christians actually arrives at the goal, at a particular way of being together in prayer, is for them and God to decide, not for anyone else.

Jesus or 'Isa?

Let's go right to the heart of what seems to prevent common prayer between Muslims and Christians by comparing what each religion actually says about Jesus — or 'Isa, as Jesus is known in the Qur'an.

A glance back at the two passages quoted above on pages 40–41 — the Qur'an's "Light Verse" and the New Testament excerpt from the beginning of the Gospel of John — will give us a starting place.

Enough has been said already to make it clear that John 1:1–5 is a major stumbling block for Muslims. The stumbling block looms not so much in the identification of Jesus with the Light, or even with the Word, since the Qur'an also calls Jesus a "word of God." The problem arises with the very different weights the two religions give these and similar terms when applied to Jesus. In John 1:1, "word" signifies God in His identity as the divine creativity who became flesh in Jesus Christ. In the Qur'an, however, "word" refers only to God's embodied teaching. The terms "word" and "spirit" when applied to God act like symbols or expressions of God's creative power and wisdom, in the same way that "light" becomes a parable of the action of God's beauty in the Qur'an's Light Verse. Word, spirit, and light are, in the Qur'an's view, manifestations of God. They are not God Himself.

So concerned is the Qur'an about what it regards as the dangerous human tendency to turn God's attributes into God's very identity that the Qur'an tries again and again to nip the tendency in the bud. A verse like the one below, explicitly forbidding what the Qur'an regards as exaggerated meanings of "word" as well as of "spirit," is typical:

> O People of the Message [Jews and particularly Christians], do not be excessive in your worship, and do not say of God anything but the truth. 'Isa Messiah, the son of Mary, was a messenger of God and God's word which he sent down upon Mary as well as a spirit from him. So believe in God and his messenger Muhammad and do not say God is a trinity, for it will be better for you. (Sura an-Nisa' 4:171)

This Qur'anic verse and others like it enforce the rejection of any Christian claim to the contrary. So when the Gospel of John 1:1 says: "and the Word was in God's presence, and the Word was God," no Muslim ever could or can now affirm such a statement.

But why not? What is the *reason* for the Qur'an's rejection?

For today's Muslims, just as for the Sultan, the identification of Jesus, or indeed of word, spirit, or light, with God is *shirk*, idolatry, the confusion of the Creator with the creature. In Islam, *shirk* is the basis of all human wrongdoing. *Shirk* is putting on the highest pedestal some ideal or goal or person, even a noble ideal or goal or person, and therefore, and necessarily, putting God second. To consider Jesus to be God is not simply, in Muslim eyes, to confuse identities. It is to lower God from His throne by bringing Him into comparison or relationship with another creature. It is even to suggest that God is not One God, but many. According to the Qur'an, the consequences of *shirk* on human behavior range from obsession to moral collapse. Having lost its basic orientation to the One God, humankind drifts toward other points on the compass, lost on the seas of illusion and need.

Christians' understanding of Jesus is obviously as different as it could possibly be. Yes, in one important respect Christians and Muslims do agree about Jesus. Along with Muslims, Christians believe that Jesus was born a human being, fully and completely so, not only physically but also in his nature — that is to say, in his entire psycho-spiritual being. But Christians also believe (a belief formalized at the Council of Chalcedon in 451) that Jesus was at the same time God. These natures, divine and human, combine without confusion in one Person, the second Person of the Trinity. This Person, with God the Father and the Holy Spirit, are the three Persons who are at the same time One God.

No Muslim ever could or ever can accept such an understanding. For Muslims, Trinitarian formulations sound deeply disrespectful of God. The formulations seem to proceed from a fantastic if not blasphemous assumption that Christians are able to see into God's very nature and to divine there a kind of absurd mathematics where the meaning of One is stood on its head. They wonder why Christians can't shelve and forget such wildly undisciplined, contentious speculations. Can't they see that to do so would be to their benefit? As the Qur'an itself says, "Do not say God is a trinity, for it will be better for you." Simple humility should dictate restraint on Christians' part, given the fact that Christianity like Islam acknowledges God's fundamental unknowability.

Yet these differing understandings of God are not so easily dismissed. They go to the heart of how Christians and Muslims experience God. The definitions take the form of propositions, but their substance is the very concrete way God manifests Himself to believers. For Muslims, God is experienced in His *tauhid*, unicity. God reigns in utter majesty above all things that are, yet in His mercy God reaches down into His creation where He is "closer than your jugular vein" (Sura Qaf 50:16). For Christians, the One God is experienced within a communion of relationships in which human creatures, through that same divine mercy, are invited to share. In Muslim understanding, God's Oneness tends to precede God's merciful relatedness with God's creatures. In a Christian understanding, God's relatedness tends to precede God's Oneness. Muslims consider 'Isa a brother in faith, uniquely gifted by God as a prophet, and therefore able to convey God's signs and favors to a weak and erring humanity. Christians consider Jesus to be the very source of those signs and favors, not merely their conveyor.

A Caution!

Exploring the similarities and differences in each other's understanding of God is not only essential. It is also stimulating and enlightening. But it can be so only if it is carried on in an open spirit. Muslims and Christians will have to keep constantly in mind that centuries of mutual polemic on this very topic — Muslim and Christian understandings of God — have muddied the waters, giving the impression that the only forms of discussion Muslims and Christians can legitimately enter into on this topic are tense and rivalrous. As we'll see in chapter 6, the assumption that Christian-Muslim discussion must necessarily be acrimonious (a verbal form of Crusade) shaped key early Christian accounts of the meeting of Francis and the Sultan at Damietta, and continues to influence certain Christian-Muslim discussions today. Muslims and Christians eager for fruitful dialogue will have to agree to watch themselves for signs of the urge to "correct" the other. Christians will be tempted to point out that the Muslim understanding of God is "deficient" because it does not include the "full" recognition of Jesus Christ's salvific identity. Muslims will be tempted to point out that the Christian understanding of God is fatally "undermined" and "adulterated" by the inclusion of humanity within divinity. Oneness

These temptations should be resisted, not in order to give tacit approval to a laissez-faire attitude toward religious truth, but to allow each other's understanding of God, and especially the experience grounding that understanding, to stand out clearly, unblemished by defensiveness. The goal Muslims and Christians seek isn't each other's doctrinal defeat or ultimate conversion, but mutual enlightenment. What *do* Christians believe about Jesus, and *why* do they believe it? These are questions that Muslims should be able to ask of Christians without fearing that the answer will come in the form of a direct attack on their own beliefs and of a follow-up effort to "convert" them. The same goes of course for Christians. What *do* Muslims believe about Jesus, and *why* do they believe it? When these questions are asked and answered in the right spirit, people usually find not only that their understanding of the Other's belief is enhanced, but also that their own belief is clarified, just by the need to express it clearly to those who sincerely seek understanding.

Comparing and Contrasting Beliefs about Jesus/ʿIsa

In preparation for the hoped-for day when we might pray to God in one voice, Muslims and Christians are urged to undertake mutual study of their respective holy books, the Qurʾan and the Bible. They can begin by comparing and contrasting passages that bear directly on contested beliefs.

For example, both the Qurʾan and the New Testament have much to say about Mary, the mother of Jesus, about the virgin birth, about the Holy Spirit, about Jesus' miracles, about Jesus' crucifixion and resurrection, and about Jesus' relation to God. They have much to say as well about other themes of mutual interest, including Creation, Adam and Eve, and the Last Judgment.

The following is an example of what can be gained for both Muslims and Christians by comparing and contrasting accounts of the "same" incident, in this case the New Testament and Qurʾanic accounts of the birth of Jesus, in the Gospel of Luke 2:3–20 and in Sura Maryam 19:22–37 respectively:

Luke 2:3–20

> ³All went to their own towns to be registered. ⁴Joseph also went from the town of Nazareth in Galilee to Judea, to the city of David called Bethlehem, because he was descended from the house and family of David. ⁵He went to be registered with Mary, to whom he was engaged and who was expecting a child. ⁶While they were there, the time came for her to deliver the child. ⁷And she gave birth to her firstborn son and wrapped him in bands of cloth and laid him in a manger, because there was no place for them in the inn.

⁸In that region there were shepherds living in the fields, keeping watch over their flock by night. ⁹Then an Angel of the Lord stood before them, and the glory of the Lord shone around them, and they were terrified. ¹⁰But then the Angel said to them, "Do not be afraid; for see — I am bringing you good news of great joy for all the people: ¹¹to you is born this day in the city of David a Savior, who is the Messiah, the Lord. ¹²This will be a sign for you: you will find the child wrapped in bands of cloth and lying in a manger." ¹³And suddenly there was with the Angel a multitude of the heavenly host, praising God and saying, ¹⁴"Glory to God in the highest heaven, and on earth peace among those whom he favors!"

¹⁵When the angels had left them and gone into heaven, the shepherds said to one another, "Let us go now to Bethlehem and see the thing that has taken place, which the Lord has made known to us." ¹⁶So they went with haste and found Mary and Joseph, and the child lying in the manger. ¹⁷When they saw this, they made known what had been told them about this child; ¹⁸and all who heard it were amazed at what the shepherds told them. ¹⁹But Mary treasured all these words and pondered them in her heart. ²⁰The shepherds returned, glorifying and praising God for all they had heard and seen, as it had been told them.

The Qur'an (Sura Maryam) [Mary] 19:22–37

²²So Mary conceived 'Isa [of the holy spirit]. Then she withdrew once more to an even more remote place. ²³Her birthpangs brought her to the shade of a date palm tree. She cried out, "Oh, how much better if I had died before this. How much better to be a thing lost and forgotten." ²⁴Just then a voice cried out from beneath the palm tree, "Don't despair, Mary, for your Cherisher and Sustainer has made a stream flow at your feet. ²⁵And shake loose some dates from the palm tree. ²⁶It will drop fresh ripe dates down for you. ²⁶Eat and drink and refresh yourself. And if you see any male stranger,

Joseph?

say, 'I have made a vow to the Merciful One to undergo a fast. Nor shall I speak this day to any human being.'"

27Once 'Isa was born, Mary brought him to her people, carrying the babe in her arms. The townspeople said, "Oh Mary, what a strange thing you've brought home! 28Oh daughter of Aaron, your father never chased after prostitutes, nor was your mother a whore." 29But instead of defending herself, Mary pointed at her child. The townspeople said, "How are we supposed to talk with a child in a cradle?" 30But the child spoke up. "Hear this," he said. "I am a servant of God. God has given me his message and has made me a prophet. 31He has made me blessed wherever I go, and he has commanded me to be faithful to prayer and almsgiving as long as I live. 32He has made me gentle and just with my mother, neither bossy nor irritable. 33So peace [*salaam*] is with me from the day of my birth to the day of my death till the day I shall be raised to life."

34Such a man was 'Isa, son of Mary. This is the truth, about which the various Christian sects vainly dispute. 35For it is not fitting that God should beget a son. Glory to God! When God decrees a matter, he only has to say of it, "Be!" — and it exists. 36Remember that God is my Cherisher and Sustainer and yours as well. So worship Him and Him alone. 37But the Christian sects differ rancorously among each other. Woe to the unbelievers at the Reckoning on that Terrible Day!

Clearly the two accounts are very different. In Luke, Jesus is born in a stable at Nazareth, where Mary and Joseph have come to register for the Roman census; in the Qur'an, Jesus is born in the desert, where Mary has fled, alone, in order to escape the shame and danger of bearing a child who has no human father. Joseph is not mentioned at all in the Qur'an's account, nor do angels and shepherds pay homage to the baby. For while both Luke and the Qur'an do refer to angelic presence at the birth of Jesus or 'Isa, the angels' function in the two accounts is not the same.

Such differences should not in themselves produce a stumbling block, however, not at least for Christians. They should know that Matthew's account of Jesus' birth also differs in its details from Luke's. For example, in Matthew 1:18–2:23, there is no mention of shepherds, while Jesus is born in a house, not a stable. Christians should not be surprised or offended, however, if Muslims view differences in the accounts of Luke and Matthew with suspicion, objecting that a story cannot be trusted if it is told in such obviously contradictory ways. Christians need to listen carefully and without defensiveness to such querying. They should keep in mind when responding to Muslim suspicions that their task is not to persuade their Muslim colleagues of the Christian viewpoint on Gospel discrepancies, but instead to clarify that viewpoint so that their Muslim colleagues can understand it, even if they don't accept it. A challenge like that is actually a very healthy one!

Christians have lived with Luke's and Matthew's nativity accounts for so long that they forget how different the accounts really are. The tradition of conflating or "harmonizing" the nativity stories in song and in devotion makes disentangling them an uncomfortable and seemingly unnecessary exercise. (How many Christians are aware that the star does not stand over the manger in Luke's account and that in fact Luke does not mention the star at all?) Christians need to ask themselves, Why is it that these discrepancies do *not* cause me to doubt the truth of the story both Luke and Matthew tell? Muslims need to hear Christians' honest efforts to answer this question and to feel free in responding to what they hear.

The real stumbling block in the Qur'anic and the biblical nativity accounts isn't found in discrepancies of detail, nor even in the different ways in which the biblical and the Qur'anic infant manifests his power: in Luke's account by occasioning angelic homage and in the Qur'anic account by defending his mother from slander while still a newborn. The real stumbling block arises with the Qur'an's assertion, in verse 35, that "it is not fitting that God should beget a son." This verse is given in explicit repudiation of the Christian claim. Does the dialogue fall down completely at this point? How can Christians and Muslims advance beyond this (Muslim) scriptural denial of (Christian) scriptural truth?

A way forward seems to open up with the word "beget." In the Qur'anic passage above, and in similar ones, it can be argued that the Qur'anic "beget" refers only to the physical act of fathering a child. Basing themselves on that interpretation, Christians can point out that they are as adamantly opposed to the literal meaning of "beget" as Muslims are! The notion of God "fathering" a son on Mary, as if the Christian God were a kind of Zeus swooping down on Leda or Io in the Greek myths, is anathema to both religions.

Christians can then show that the meaning they attribute to "beget" is as far as possible from the literal meaning. Especially in the form "only begotten," an adjective reverently attached to Jesus five times in the Gospel of John and enshrined as well in the Nicene-Constantinoplan Creed of 381 (the most widely used of all Christian creeds), "beget" means God's eternal act of issuing Himself from Himself as Word in creative love. The result of this unique act of begetting is His "only begotten Son": not a being or creation separate from Himself but His own self created in and for relationship within God's own Oneness but also outwardly with the created world. This meaning is the one expressed in a verse from the Gospel of John that for many Christians is the heart of the entire Gospel: "For God so loved the world, that He gave His only begotten Son, that whoever believes in Him may not perish, but have eternal life" (John 3:16).

So have Christians found a way to avoid the stumbling block of Jesus' relation to God? Can the dispute over the identity of Jesus be relegated to the level of misunderstanding?

No, unfortunately the dispute cannot be disposed of in this way. For the Qur'an's use of "beget" is broad enough to include the actual Christian meaning, the meaning enshrined in the adjective "only begotten." "Beget" is just as objectionable to Muslims in its spiritual sense as it is in its literal sense for a reason already stated: for its implication that human beings really can see deeply into God's own nature. To do so, or to claim to be able to do so, is for human beings to arrogate to themselves a kind of equality with God. Human beings must understand and respect their creaturely limits. As the Qur'an states, "Human vision does not grasp and contain God; rather, God grasps and contains human vision, for God is the Most Subtle, the Most Knowing" (Sura An'am 6:103)

Yet Christians would earnestly protest that their belief in God as Trinity is not mere human insight. They would argue that it is a truth revealed to them by God through scripture and their experience of the risen Christ. As a result, they too can claim allegiance to the Qur'anic statement above. For doesn't Christian scripture say, "No one has seen God" (John 1:18; 1 John 4:12)? Christians no more pretend to equality with God than Muslims do.

So near and yet so far. Christians and Muslims repeatedly find themselves at one moment standing side by side as believers in the One God. At another moment an impassable gulf seems to yawn between them.

Yet does acknowledging this fact mean that to continue to dialogue about God, in the hopes of praying in common to God, is a futile exercise?

No, it does not, for what might seem the absurdly self-evident reason that God is too important to be kept in the background. What Christians and Muslims actually believe about God is perhaps less important than how they hold those beliefs: with anxious defensiveness or with openness, joy, and wonder. God is not the head of a Muslim or a Christian tribe. God is the maker of heaven and earth, and while the forms of God's revelations to Muslims and Christians appear seriously to contradict each other at certain points, that circumstance cannot possibly hold the whole truth about God. Perhaps the contradictions are not stumbling blocks at all but God's way of stimulating deeper penetration into God's mystery. Muslims and Christians truly in love with God, as their religions call them to be, will not be afraid to enter that mystery with each other.

The Lord's Prayer and the Fatihah as Points of Entry

Two points of entry that Muslims and Christians can test out together are those provided by the prayers each community regularly uses both in their respective worship gatherings and in private worship. These are the Lord's Prayer and the Fatihah, or Opening, the first of the Qur'an's suras. The prayers are comparable in structure and brevity. Both are prayers given by God to humankind, as guides for the way humankind should address God and for the things it should ask of Him. Despite these similarities, however, we still have to ask: Does either prayer contain an insuperable stumbling block for the person of the other faith?

The Lord's Prayer (Gospel of Matthew 6:9–13)

Our Father, who art in heaven, hallowed be your name.

Your kingdom come, your will be done, on earth as it is in heaven.

Give us this day our daily bread.

And forgive us our trespasses, as we forgive those who trespass against us.

Lead us not into temptation, but deliver us from evil. Amen.

The Fatihah (Sura Fatihah 1:1–7)

In the name of God, the Most Beneficent, the Most Merciful.

All praise to God, Cherisher and Sustainer of the worlds

The Most Beneficent, the Most Merciful.

Presider over the Day of Judgment.

To you we come as servants, to you we cry for help.

Lead us along the straight path,

The Path of those to whom you have given your favor, not of those for whom

there is wrath or who have gone astray. Amen.

The more one studies these prayers, the more similar they look. Both prayers begin by addressing and praising God; they then affirm the peoples' desire to live in conformity with God's will for them; they end with petitions, first for God's favor and guidance and then for protection against destruction. The prayers are concluded with the same word, "amen" (*ameen* in Arabic), signifying the worshiping community's assent to what it has just said and its confidence in God's merciful attention.

Can Christians pray the Fatihah with Muslims? Yes, it appears that they can. For though the name of Jesus is not mentioned in the Fatihah, neither is it mentioned in the Lord's Prayer. In terms of *iman*, or belief, there is nothing said about God in the Fatihah that contracts Christian understanding. God's benevolence, God's mercy, God's concern to sustain what God has created, God's role at Judgment — these are qualities and capacities Christians ascribe to God as fervently as Muslims do. Similarly with the Fatihah's characterization of humanity's proper responses to such a God: their desire that God's will be theirs and their confidence that He will hear them in their distress. Christians can also appreciate a prayer asking for God's favor or grace. They too understand their lives as journeys or pilgrimages where through defiance or carelessness they can come to grief. So the conclusion seems clear: nothing in the prayer itself seems to be a stumbling block for Christians.

What of the Lord's Prayer for Muslims? Can Muslims feel at home in it as quickly as Christians seem to be able to do with the Fatihah?

The answer is: No, they can't. There may be no insuperable barrier to Muslims' praying the Lord's Prayer (no mention of Jesus as God's Son, for example), but there are rocky stretches. Perhaps the chief of them looms up right away: God as Father. Because of Islam's attitude toward idolatry, all language seeming to endow God with explicit human characteristics is prohibited. Accordingly, Qur'anic terms suggesting that God has a body or occupies space (sitting on a "throne," for example, as in the Qur'an's "Throne Verse," Sura al-Baqarah 2:255) are considered strictly symbolic. And while English versions of the Qur'an regularly employ the masculine pronoun "He" for God, the masculine pronoun carries no implication of gender.

Under the light of such prohibitions, a term like "Father" seems to bring God too close.

It is not the case, though, that Muslims regard God as incapable or undesirous of intimacy with his human creation. It is rather that the intimacy is God's, not ours, to name. The Qur'anic verse "When my servants ask about me, tell them that I am near. I respond to the cry of all who cry out to me" (Sura al-Baqarah 2:186) certainly suggests a parental relationship with humanity on God's part, even if God does not name Himself as parent. Accordingly, while Muslims might feel uneasy using the name "Father" of God, there appears to be no insuperable difficulty in their doing so.

Yet even if the language of the Lord's Prayer and the Fatihah can be shown to contain no impossible impediment to common prayer on the part of Muslims and Christians, there is a further objection that has to be faced. The objection is based on the fact that these prayers do not exist in a vacuum. The prayers do not begin and end with the words actually used in them. The Fatihah and the Lord's Prayer are deeply imbedded within the scriptures and worship traditions of the communities that draw life from them. They therefore carry in them unstated meanings that are clarified by their contexts. The Fatihah, for example, serves as both the introduction to and the epitome of the rest of the Qur'an, which follows after it. So while the Fatihah itself says nothing about Jesus, it tacitly affirms what is said about Jesus elsewhere in the Qur'an and in Muslim tradition. The same is true of the Lord's Prayer. While the Lord's Prayer makes no explicit claim about Jesus as God's Son, it tacitly affirms what is revealed about Jesus in the New Testament and throughout Christian tradition.

And beyond even that, the Fatihah and the Lord's Prayer affirm not only differing understandings of Jesus, but differing understandings on a host of other themes and issues. Which is only to say the obvious, that the two prayers belong to their own respective religious traditions and to no other.

How can a Christian pray the Fatihah without thereby becoming Muslim? How can a Muslim pray the Our Father without thereby becoming Christian?

If *islam* (outward practices) and *iman* (beliefs) were all, they could not.

That still leaves *ihsan* (spirituality).

Does *ihsan* provide an avenue toward having prayer in common? Does *ihsan* provide an entrance into what we spoke of above as the "mystery" of our relationship with God, a relationship that neither Christianity nor Islam can fully define and own?

Looking Forward

Testing together whether it is possible to pray to God as one community from within that mystery is the true goal of Christians and Muslims. Whether they reach this goal at any particular time by praying their separate prayers side-by-side or by praying in one voice is less important than fidelity to the quality of their experience as it unfolds. Christians and Muslims hope someday to be able to pray in one voice, because all humanity is one under One God. But if Christians and Muslims arrive at their goal of common prayer, they'll do so because they have understood how to keep the tension between their faiths at its most creative pitch. Muslims will intimately know, during such prayer, the sacrifice their Christian colleagues are making by *not* mentioning Jesus' name. Or maybe the sacrifice will belong to the Muslims. They will submit themselves to a prayer through a Jesus who is God only for the Other, but they do so in respect for a belief deeply held by their colleagues.

Muslims and Christians so engaged might seem to be going through the same motions and saying the same things as those who rushed into prayer in one voice right at the start of their relationship. But the quality of their prayer will be different. In the first case, where Muslims and Christians unite around love of the mystery, the prayer will be tentative, humbly aware of human imperfection and finitude, yet eagerly watchful and hopeful. In the second case, where prayer in one voice is jumped into, it will become pro forma, an easy and even self-congratulating sign of a solidarity that has not been struggled for.

If Francis and the Sultan were with us today, which option would most attract them? Muslims and Christians have an equal stake in answering that question.

Discussion Questions

1. What are the challenges for Muslims and Christians who want to pray in one voice to the One God in whom they both believe?

2. Why is it important to maintain a creative tension around the question of praying together?

3. Christians and Muslims view Jesus/'Isa in very different ways. Explain these differences.

4. How has the discussion of the two birth narratives presented in this chapter altered your understanding of the birth of Jesus/'Isa?

5. Do you believe it is appropriate for a Muslim to pray the Lord's Prayer or for a Christian to pray the Muslim Fatihah? Explain.

Part II

Reviewing Each Other's Spiritual Warrants for Social Justice Ministry

Chapter 3

THE FUNDAMENTALS
OF CHRISTIAN SOCIAL JUSTICE

Francis and Peacemaking

Let's stop for a moment and try to recall how unusual this meeting between Francis and the Sultan actually was.

Here we have two people divided by war and religion (and the lethal mixing of the two), yet taking advantage of a shaky truce on the field of battle to meet in peace and for peace.

Francis approached his meeting with Sultan Malik intending to convert the Sultan to Christianity. He hoped by that means not only to save the Sultan's soul, but also to achieve the peace that warfare showed no sign of establishing. Yet Francis did not set about evangelizing in the usual aggressive way. The evidence suggests that Francis's approach was very different from one of anxiety to prove himself and his religion "right." His spirit was spontaneous and open to exchange. He was genuinely curious about the Sultan's religion. This curiosity obviously had nothing to do with dissatisfaction on Francis's part with his own faith or with a desire to "convert" to the other's. It had rather to do with the opposite motive: the desire to understand. Francis's confidence in his own way of worship was deep enough to free him from defensiveness and from the need to triumph over his "opponent." It was deep enough as well to allow him to explore the mystery of God's communication with all God's creatures, not just with those of a particular faith. Francis's openness was a product of his own prior spiritual formation. But it was matched by a reciprocal curiosity and openness displayed by the Sultan.

The resulting discussion almost certainly took the form of a debate, for that was the style of intellectual give-and-take in those days. (We'll trace the probable course of their discussion in chapter 7.) But the goal of the debate was not to come away with a trophy of victory. The goal, a goal embraced as warmly by the Sultan as by Francis, was to offer the fruit of their meeting to the God who seeks the well-being of every one of His creatures, and who expects those creatures to treat each other with a mercy not unlike God's own.

Neither Francis nor the Sultan dreamed up this goal right there during their actual meeting on the battlefield at Damietta. Rather, they came to the meeting already deeply committed to their religions' common command that they be peacemakers. The key question for us in the present chapter is, What prompted this commitment? Something in their previous experience had enabled them to work through the smoke of prejudice and violence to a clear view of what following Jesus' or Muhammad's footsteps really meant: not doctrinal rigidity but nonjudgmental fellowship with all God's creatures.

Let's start with the first question, asking it first of Francis. Let's go back in time to the roots of his development into a proponent and exemplar of Christian peacemaking.

How Francis Became St. Francis

Like many of the upper-class young men of his time, Francis started out enjoying the benefits of his status and dreaming of becoming a knight. When his hometown of Assisi went to war with the neighboring city of Perugia, Francis enthusiastically joined the small army as a mounted soldier. But the Perugian army routed the army from Assisi. Francis watched in horror as his fleeing friends were hunted down like animals. He himself was taken prisoner rather than slaughtered because, as the son of wealthy merchant, he could be ransomed for a generous reward. After a year in an underground prison, he emerged a broken human being. Francis was too weak to leave his father's house. Once a carefree young man, he was now depressed. He walked with a cane.

After healing from his physical injuries, Francis tried again to fulfill his dream of becoming a knight, for this was an age when war making was a dominant cultural fixation. He signed up with the papal forces to fight a war in the southern Italian town of Apulia. Yet while heading south to join the battle, he became uneasy. Not far from Assisi in Spoleto, he had a dream in which he heard God's voice telling him to turn back from the path of war. He wheeled his horse around and headed home. But by turning around, Francis was rejecting not only war. He was also rejecting the Crusades, for crusading colored even local disputes. Pope Innocent III had granted Crusade privileges to those who fought in the war in Apulia. ("Crusade privileges" included remission of sins for those who undertook a Crusade for devotion's sake rather than for gain or fame.) And the leader of the pope's army, Walter of Brienne, was planning to continue on with his band of men to fight in the Fourth Crusade in the Holy Land.

Upon his return to Assisi, Francis sold his horse, his weaponry, and his clothing and gave everything to the poor. He began a new chapter in his life, embracing radical poverty and penance. He began to repair churches, which was one way that military men atoned for their sins on the battlefield.

By rejecting his former way of life and the world it represented — greed, violence, and war — Francis discovered another. He attached himself to the words and actions of the nonviolent and poor Jesus. Francis could see plainly that the greed dominating his society was directly linked to the pervasive violence of war. For him voluntary poverty and peacemaking were linked.

Francis entered into a radical companionship with the poor and, through them, with all creation. The poor reminded him of his true nature, that of a dependent creature, far from the image of proud, aggressive, self-sufficient mastery projected and promoted by his culture. For Francis, poverty was "a way of being by which the individual lets things be what they are; one refuses to dominate them, subjugate them, and make them objects of the will to power."[1]

Because the desire for possessions stands between people's true communication with each other and with all creation, Francis let go of this desire. As Francis became poorer, he became more fraternal; he saw poverty as the way into the experience of universal fraternity with all creation. He realized that he was a creature among creatures, a fellow companion with all the rest of creation. He was not "over things, but with them, like brothers and sisters of the same family."[2]

This realization was not a sentimental "feel good" indulgence on the part of Francis, or an exaggeratedly idealistic one. It was based on Jesus' own words, especially in the Sermon on the Mount: "But I say to you, love your enemies, and pray for those who persecute you." Francis repeated this verse four times in the small collection of his known writings. For example, in his *Earlier Rule,* he explained that since Jesus had called Judas, who betrayed him, friend, therefore we are to call our friends those "who give us trouble and suffering." Some scholars, like Franciscan scholar David Flood, believe that the above passage from the Sermon on the Mount was a parting testament that Francis delivered to his followers before leaving for Egypt to encounter the Sultan. Paul Moses considers it an explanation for why he risked his life once he arrived there: he wanted to befriend his enemy, the "infidel" Muslim.[3]

The Christian Calling to Peacemaking and Social Justice

We've just reviewed some of the steps that led to the transformation of Francis from a man of war to a man of peace. Francis did not begin life as "St. Francis." He was shaped by the aggressive spirit of his age and by a church that had co-opted that spirit in order to promote and foster a Crusade not only against Muslim "infidels" but also against all others (such as pagans and heretics) who opposed the church's rule. It took a severe shock, the trauma of war, to begin to free Francis from this spirit's spell. But the shock didn't simply destroy that spell. It opened him to the influence of another kind of spirit, the Holy Spirit. Under this Spirit's influence, Francis was able to rebuild his identity and redirect his life. He was able to give expression to a version of his faith that was rooted in a radical (in the literal sense of the most deeply "rooted") understanding of Christianity. He did this by taking the words of Jesus at face value, the words rejecting worldly possessions and violence. Francis found his bearings in Jesus' explicit commands to "love your enemy" and care for the "least of these." And it was with this understanding of himself and of his religion that he approached the Sultan's tent.

A Pause for Reflection

Today's Christians and Muslims hoping to follow in the footsteps of Francis and the Sultan should take time before they go any further to look back at their understandings of themselves and of their religions. They should ask themselves: How did I learn of my own religion's peacemaking and social justice traditions? Was my path to this understanding — a path that could lead me to join with members of the "enemy" religion in solidarity with the poor of the world — was my path as dangerous and troubled as that of Francis? A self-reflection of this kind entails a review of the foundations of peacemaking and social justice in both traditions. (We'll be reviewing Christian social justice foundations here in this third chapter and Muslim foundations in the fourth.) But the main point of the present chapter and the next is to help Christians and Muslims decide how strongly they affirm these foundations, first in their own religion and then in the religion of the Other.

Why is there something to decide here? Because affirming peacemaking foundations can get you in trouble! Our present-day world culture is arguably just as warlike as the culture of Francis's day, and some contemporary branches of both Christianity and Islam espouse a militancy little different from the Holy War mentality of Pope Urban II. Today's Christians and Muslims need to be conscious of the price one sometimes pays for initiating missions of peace in a world too often bent on initiating missions of just the opposite sort. Christians and Muslims also need to reflect on the fact that many of their fellow practitioners are simply ignorant not only of their faith's peacemaking and social justice foundations, but also of the traditions based upon them. (In chapter 7 we'll be examining those traditions, especially in their present-day updatings.) For example, Roman Catholics possess a rich source of social justice teachings going back over a century. But Roman Catholics who have studied these teachings often refer to them, ruefully, as "the Catholic Church's best kept secret," since so few people in the pews have heard of them. So the question is: Are Christians and Muslims willing to take the responsibility of educating their fellow practitioners in their respective social justice foundations and traditions? Their mutual commitment should be firm. The success of any interfaith effort to promote social justice begins with helping members of one's own faith see that social justice is not a "foreign import," but a basic mandate of their own religion, whether Christian or Muslim.

Hearing What Each Other Says about Social Justice

Even though we are presenting in this chapter the fundamentals of the Christian social justice tradition, we do so as if Muslims were listening over our shoulder. It is not enough for Christians alone to be reminded of these fundamentals (or to hear about them for the first time!). If members of both religions are to work together to promote a social justice agenda, they need to be aware of each other's social justice traditions. They also need to have the opportunity to respond to and, yes, sometimes to critique the terms in which the other religion presents these fundamentals to its own members.

Of course the same logic applies to Muslims' reminding each other of their own fundamentals. That's why we will pursue the same method in the next chapter, presenting Muslim fundamentals as if Christians were listening over our shoulder. Neither

Muslims nor Christians should be passive observers of such explanations. Rather, they should be active participants in a discussion that should prove all the more enlightening for being taken up from different perspectives.

Having the Other in the audience as Christians hear their social justice foundations presented has an immediate benefit. Since peacemaking is such a key part of social justice, and since Muslims have often been in past centuries Christians' sworn enemies, Christians will be forced to distinguish between what their own faith *teaches* about peacemaking and how they have in fact *behaved*. This act of intellectual honesty must be met by Muslims with honesty about similar discrepancies between their own ideals and practices. Muslims should also be ready to acknowledge moments where Christian social justice fundamentals supply an insight hitherto invisible to them into their own social justice traditions. Both religions have everything to gain and nothing to lose by reviewing their social justice commitments through each other's eyes.

Similarly, when we talk about the Muslim social justice tradition in chapter 4, Muslims will need to be honest about the discrepancies between their own ideals and practices. And Christians will need to acknowledge those moments where the Muslim understanding of social justice opens up aspects of their own tradition that they hadn't seen before — aspects taken for granted, perhaps, or obscured by custom or distorted by bias.

Christian Social Justice Traditions

Beginning in Scripture

Our presentation of the Christian social justice tradition begins where Francis found his inspiration, in the Bible. The key text for this purpose is the Sermon on the Mount from the Gospel of Matthew, chapters 5 through 7, with particular attention to the passages from the Sermon on the Mount most directly cited and acted upon by Francis himself: Matthew 5:3–12 (the Beatitudes),

5:21–26 (against anger), 5:38–48 (against revenge and for love of enemy), and 6:16–25 (on fasting and poverty).

Jesus' insistence on peacemaking ("Blessed also are the Peacemakers" in Matthew 5:9) was neither a new idea for his Jewish co-religionists nor a hobbyhorse of his own but a deeply rooted element of the Jewish religion itself. The stress on peacemaking follows from the two most repeated themes both in the Hebrew scriptures (Old Testament) and in the Christian scriptures (New Testament). Those two themes are God's warnings against idolatry and God's urgent appeal for concern for the poor, an appeal that reflects God's abhorrence of injustice. Again and again God warns humankind through the prophets that idolatry breeds injustice and that injustice inevitably issues in violence. That is because all three evils are rooted in denial of God and of the sacredness of creation.

God's Warnings against Idolatry and God's Concern for the Poor

Idolatry and injustice follow from one another and are often linked in scriptural accounts. In the New Testament, one out of every sixteen verses connects poverty with the abuse of wealth (Mammon, as the Gospels call it). In the Gospels of Matthew and Mark, it is one out of every ten verses. In the Gospel of Luke, God's concern for those who are poor is found in one in every seven verses![4]

God's Initiative to Promote Peacemaking: Covenant

God's warnings against idolatry and His expressions of concern for the poor are not isolated assertions on God's part. They originate in God's prior covenants with humankind.

The covenants are agreements which God initiates and to which God promises to be faithful, while people are expected to keep their side of the agreement, by obeying God's commands. In the biblical account (including both Old and New Testaments), God made four covenants: with Noah after the flood, with Abraham and Sarah, with Moses and the Hebrews in the desert at Mt. Sinai, and with Jesus and his disciples. We'll treat just the last two here, beginning with the third covenant with Moses and the Hebrews at Sinai.

This covenant, expressed in the Ten Commandments, details God's initiative with the people as well as the terms of the people's proper response. The Sinai covenant calls on the community to reject idolatry and to accept only Yahweh as their God, and it tells the community how they are to treat the poor and marginalized: the widow, the orphan, and the resident alien. God also gives the people a land where they can thrive. In covenant making, God takes the initiative. It is *God's work.* In the Bible God is forever creating, restoring when broken, and completing in the end time a *covenant community* whose main characteristics are peace and justice.[5]

The biblical prophets called the Israelite community back to the requirements of the covenant when greed and idolatry led them to disregard it. Jesus continued and broadened the message of the prophets by announcing a new covenant that would be open to all people, not just the Israelites and their descendants, the Jews. The Spirit of God pushes the community of all believers in Christ's resurrection (called the "church") to be faithful to the covenant of Jesus in every age and in every circumstance. This new covenant ("new testament") grounds the church's social mission in the very work of God. The church is called to continue God's work in the world.

The pervasive biblical focus on covenant community does not fit easily with the Western emphasis on individual rights, as Roman Catholic scripture scholar John Donahue points out:

> In contrast to modern individualism the Israelite is in a world where "to live" is to be united with others in a social context either by bonds of family or by covenant relationships. This web of relationships — king with people, judge with complainants, family with tribe and kinfolk, the community with the resident alien and suffering in their midst

and all with the covenant God — constitutes the world in which life is played out.[6]

Such a communitarian social context is found in traditional cultures that are not foreign either to Christian or to Muslim communities in developing countries. The balancing of the needs of the individual and the community is a complex and difficult task in any culture, but it has proved especially difficult in modern cultures driven by individualism.

Biblical Rights and Responsibilities

As the U.S. Declaration of Independence puts it, human rights are the "inalienable rights of each person." Rights belong to the individual. Biblical rights are different. The biblical notion of rights and responsibilities flows from the relationships that are part of living in community. This assertion of human rights as a communal rather than an individual good is at the heart of the covenant that God established with the Hebrews and all people. The Hebrew word that is used to express that aspect of the covenant is *sedaqah,* which is translated as justice or righteousness. Hebrew scripture scholar Gerard von Rad writes: "There is absolutely no concept in the Old Testament with so central a significance for all relationships of human life as that of *sedaqah* [justice/righteousness]."[7]

A pivotal expression of *sedaqah* is the experience of the Exodus. Scripture scholar Walter Brueggemann explains that *sedaqah*

> . . . as hoped for by Israel, resisted by Pharaoh, and finally given by Yahweh is not simply a retributive arrangement whereby each receives what is "deserved," but rather a radical notion of distributive practice that gives to each one what is needed — by way of legitimacy, dignity, power, and wherewithal — in order to live a life of well-being.[8]

In this new *sedaqah* of God each person is a valued "end" of God, not a "means" to someone else's wealth. The Passover vision of *sedaqah* presents God, the creator of heaven and earth, "as the active agent in the reshaping of human social power for the sake of human community and well-being."[9] Clearly, scripture and human rights are rooted in a communal consciousness.

The Christian Challenge, Then and Now

When Francis began to take the words of Jesus at face value, rejecting worldly possessions and violence, loving his enemy, and caring for the "least of these," he was challenging the dominant medieval interpretation of Christianity. "Christendom," as the social and political expression of that interpretation, represented the uneasy balance of power between church and worldly princes with the church often legitimating the actions of the princes and lords. But we now see he was doing so for reasons that reach back into the history of the Jewish people and particularly into the story of their relationship to God through covenant.

What Francis added to this understanding of covenant was greater emphasis on the link between idolatry and possessiveness and on the corresponding link between covenant faithfulness and voluntary poverty. He did not create these links where none existed before, however. He found them embodied in the person and behavior of the Jesus of the Gospels. What's more, he brought this Jesus to life in his own teaching and example — or in his own teaching *through* example, for Francis is famous for urging his followers to "preach constantly, and sometimes even in words!" The church is forever indebted to Francis for restoring to all Christians the vision of true Christian covenant faithfulness.

Foundations of Christian Social Justice: Against Idolatry and Possessiveness

The Bible as a whole is not a rulebook even though we find rules, such as the Ten Commandments, within its pages. The Bible is better seen as "a body of witnesses to what it means to live a human life before a creating, sustaining, and saving God."[10] Professor Luke Timothy Johnson explains that when we look at the

Bible in this way, we find "a great deal being said about the way people use possessions." The Bible's focus is not so much on the things themselves as "what they mean for those who claimed them." Johnson believes that our attitude toward possessions is either one of idolatry or true faith — a stark choice indeed! Our response to possessions tells us what we perceive as of ultimate value in our lives. Possessions become an idol if they enslave worshipers of "the true God who calls humans out of such fearful, compulsive self-grasping into a new life of freedom that enables them to use things without being owned by them." He goes on to say that "The first and most fundamental meaning of possessions, then, is their expression of the human response of idolatry or faith before the mystery of existence."[11] Of course many in the West today dismiss the idea of idolatry, associating the practice with barbaric rites performed before hideous statues in remote times and places. They see themselves as an "advanced," "enlightened" people, a race highly raised above such remote, distasteful origins. To prick our bubble and disabuse us of such self-congratulatory comparisons, Johnson translates the meaning of idolatry into contemporary language: "Idolatry, in simple terms, is the choice of treating as ultimate and absolute that which is neither absolute nor ultimate. We treat something as ultimate by the worship we pay it." Worship in this context is not the worship of our lips or standing at the altar with incense, but the worship of service. Worship is service. Hence, my god is that which I serve. "Whatever I may claim as ultimate, the truth is that my god is that which rivets my attention, centers my activity, preoccupies my mind, and motivates my action." That for which I give up anything else is my god.[12]

The Gospel of Luke is particularly rich in its illustrations of idolatry. One such illustration comes from the parable of the rich man with the barns.

> And [Jesus] said to them, "Take care! Be on your guard against all kinds of greed; for one's life does not consist in

the abundance of possessions." Then he told them a parable: "The land of a rich man produced abundantly. And he thought to himself, 'What should I do, for I have no place to store my crops?' Then he said, 'I will do this: I will pull down my barns and build larger ones, and there I will store all my grain and my goods. And I will say to my soul, "Soul, you have ample goods laid up for many years; relax, eat, drink, and be merry."' But God said to him, 'You fool! This very night your life is being demanded of you; and the things you have prepared, whose will they be?' So it is with those who store up treasures for themselves but are not rich toward God." (Luke 12:15–21)

Johnson comments that Jesus explicitly and emphatically rejects the identification of "life" with "abundance of possessions." The man in the parable is not a fool because he is rich. "He is a fool because he identifies his very existence with the security he thinks comes from having grain stored in barns." He has made the mistake of equating his life, his being, with what he has. Rather than realizing his life is in God's hands he trusts in his possessions. This man identifies his life with his possessions. He identifies his being with his having, which is a fatal mistake. The Bible teaches us to trust only in God, but we are tempted to trust in our possessions or some other god.

Sharing Possessions

But if possessions themselves are morally neutral and if hoarding them is idolatry, what is the right attitude toward them, since it's clear that right or wrong resides in the attitude rather than in the object?

Johnson holds up an ethic of sharing rather than of ownership. For how can we truly "own" what has come from God and must return to God? "The mandate of faith in God is clear: we must, in some fashion, share that which has been given to us by God as a gift. To refuse to share what we have is to act idolatrously." Johnson gives us an image that expresses our too-often indulged and ultimately self-destructive attitude toward God and our possessions: a clenched hand:

> The significance of the sharing of possessions, whether by once-for-all donation or by steady almsgiving or by a community of goods...expresses our self-disposition toward God and the world. The clenched hand, the stance of holding and hoarding our possessions...manifests and makes real our closure against God and the world. The open hand, the sharing of possessions,...reveals and makes actual our availability to God and the world.[13]

Johnson points out that there is no one way to share our possessions. Sharing is not a matter of following a simple formula, but the result of creative insight into each other's true needs and priorities. Nor does sharing pertain only to physical objects. For just as we can be possessive of our talents, time, and energy (and thereby turn them into idols), we can be generous with them as well.

Jesus as Exemplar of What It Means to Share

Jesus' own behavior sets the gold standard for a nonidolatrous attitude toward possessions. Here are just a few of the Gospel passages that bear this truth out:

* Jesus' feeding of thousands of his poor and hungry followers through a sharing of the few available loaves and fishes (Matthew 14:13–21; Mark 6:32–44; Luke 9:10–17; John 6:1–15).

* Jesus' sharing in the lives of those who are poor, a practice that sometimes resulted in his having no roof over his head (Matthew 8:20; Luke 9:58).

* Jesus' sharing of his gifts of healing with all who seek them (too many references to list here!).

* Jesus' sharing in the burdens and miseries of human life to the extent of suffering death on a cross.

The early church took to heart Jesus' example of sharing and absorbed it as an essential dimension of their faith. Two passages from the Acts of the Apostles express this dimension:

> They devoted themselves to the apostles' teaching and fellowship, to the breaking of bread and the prayers. Awe came upon everyone, because many wonders and signs were being done by the apostles. All who believed were together and had all things in common; they would sell their possessions and goods and distribute the proceeds to all, as any had need. Day by day, as they spent much time together in the temple, they broke bread at home and ate their food with glad and generous hearts, praising God and having the goodwill of all the people. (Acts 2:42–47)

> Now the whole group of those who believed were of one heart and one soul, and no one claimed private ownership of any possessions, but everything they owned was held in common. With great power the apostles gave their testimony to the resurrection of the Lord Jesus, and great grace was upon them all. There was not a needy person among them, for as many as owned lands or houses sold them and brought the proceeds of what was sold. They laid it at the apostles' feet, and it was distributed to each as any had need. (Acts 4:32–35)

This picture of a community that shares all, so that the needs of all would be met, is an ideal picture, an image of sharing by which later communities could judge themselves.[14] But clearly the members of the early church saw themselves as living out the reality of covenant. The phrase in Acts 4:34, "there was none needy among them," is a reference to Deuteronomy 15:4, which promised that when the laws of almsgiving were perfectly kept there would be no more needy persons. Luke, the author of the Acts of the Apostles, is suggesting that the first Christian community, inspired by Jesus' example and the power of the Holy Spirit, fulfilled the Jewish desire for a community without poverty.

"You Always Have the Poor with You"

In Mark 14:7 Jesus says, "for you always have the poor with you, and you can show kindness to them whenever you wish." Some have interpreted these words to mean that Christians should just accept poverty as reality and not try to change the situation. Professor Johnson interprets Jesus' words differently. His interpretation, drawn from the Hebrew scriptures, takes the form of a question: *Why* are the poor always with us? The answer Johnson gives, drawn again from the Hebrew scriptures, is this: The poor are always with you because there is always the ruling class that takes advantage of the people of the land.

Jesus does not mean, in other words, that you always have the poor with you because the poor consist of lazy, unemployed, "welfare moms" who pass their idleness on to their offspring, who pass it on to theirs, and so on ad infinitum. Nor does Jesus mean that God *wants* the poor to suffer through the ages. Rather, Jesus is offering a sad commentary on the persistence of greed and exploitation, and on the poverty and violence entailed by the exploitation itself.

So when Jesus made the comment above, about always having the poor with you, he was probably remembering a certain passage from Deuteronomy, the one that imagines the day when

> there will . . . be no one in need among you, because the Lord is sure to bless you in the land that the Lord your God is giving you as a possession to occupy, if only you will obey the Lord your God by diligently observing this entire commandment that I command you today. (Deuteronomy 15:4–6)

Jesus was probably contrasting the vision described in that passage with the sad reality he knew only too well: the reality of the breaking of the covenant by the elites and of the inevitable result of that transgression — poverty and violence. In this light, Jesus' comment that "you always have the poor with you" could reflect his melancholy assessment of the enduring quality of human evil.

Or more likely it reflects a kind of "divine irony," allowing those of his listeners who would catch his reference to the passage in Deuteronomy the chance to make the contrast for themselves and to draw their own conclusions. For all would know, rich and poor alike, that poverty violates the intention of God's covenant. God's plan is that "there will be *no* one in need among you." But since the elites have violated God's covenant, injustice and the violence of poverty abound. The proof of covenant-breaking is painfully inescapable in the evidence of human misery.[15]

From Peacemaking to Nonviolence

Nonviolence as practiced by Mahatma Gandhi and Dr. Martin Luther King Jr. is a modern development. As a spiritual orientation and as a method for asserting human rights it has roots in many religious traditions, not just in Christian tradition. But it is certainly central there. Jesus himself embodies nonviolence. He does so by renouncing violence as a strategy for promoting God's kingdom." Scripture scholar Richard Hays explains:

> The evangelists are unanimous in portraying Jesus as a Messiah who subverts all prior expectations by assuming the vocation of suffering rather than conquering Israel's enemies. Despite his stinging criticism of those in positions of authority, he never attempts to exert force as a way of gaining social or political power.[16]

Hays argues further that "there is not a syllable in the Pauline letters that can be cited in support of Christians employing violence." In other words, "from Matthew to Revelation *we find a consistent witness against violence* and a calling to the community to follow the example of Jesus in accepting suffering rather than inflicting it."[17] Roman Catholic moral theologian Lisa Sowle Cahill concurs that "nothing is more clear in the moral message of Jesus than his exhortation to and example of forgiveness, mercy, and meekness in the face of abuse or assault."[18]

A number of Christian denominations such as the Mennonites, the Brethren, and the Society of Friends (Quakers) have given a more consistent witness to the nonviolence of Jesus than have the mainline Protestant and Catholic churches. But in more recent times these communities too have begun to reclaim a commitment to peace-building and nonviolence. In their 1983 Pastoral Letter *The Challenge of Peace,* the U.S. Catholic bishops reminded Catholics that "Peacemaking is not an optional commitment. It is a requirement of our faith. We are called to be peacemakers, not by some movement of the moment, but by our Lord Jesus" (#332). Pope John Paul II spoke clearly against war in general and the first Gulf War specifically:

> No, never again war, which destroys the lives of innocent people, teaches how to kill, throws into upheaval even the lives of those who do the killing and leaves behind a trail of resentment and hatred, thus making it all the more difficult to find a just solution of the very problems which provoked the war. (*Centesimus Annus,* 52)

Father Thomas Merton, a Trappist monk, reminds Christians of the task before them. "Christ our Lord did not come to bring peace as a kind of spiritual tranquilizer. He brought to his disciples a vocation and task: to struggle in the world of violence to establish His peace not only in their own hearts but in society itself."[19]

More recently, Monsignor William Shannon has directed us to find the core of Merton's nonviolent project in a vision that reflects Francis's own:

> We shall only learn to deal effectively with violence when we discover (or recover, for it is really always there) in ourselves that contemplative awareness that enables us — as it had enabled Merton — to see the oneness we share with all God's people — indeed with the whole of God's creation.

Shannon continues:

Once a person has achieved this contemplative insight, non-violence ceases to be a mere option and becomes a choice that brooks no rejection. But let no one think that becoming nonviolent is an easy task. It calls for painful, ongoing conversion, as slowly and almost imperceptibly we begin to realize what it asks of us and to experience the wisdom it imparts to us.[20]

Catholics, and Protestants too, have much to thank figures like Fathers Merton and Shannon for helping them recover an orientation that had become obscured by centuries of aggression tragically and sinfully carried out in the name of the poor and nonviolent Jesus.

Voluntary Poverty: Jesus' Influence on Francis

We return to Francis, and especially to Francis's decision back in Assisi to sell his horse, his weaponry, and his clothing and give everything to the poor. The behavior that shocked and angered his father and many other "good Christians" of Assisi now should look completely understandable. Francis was simply bypassing "Christianity" in the form in which his culture had presented it to him in order to unite himself directly to Jesus himself. Undoubtedly Francis undertook this project solely for personal motives. He was not at first looking to save any other soul than his own. But several factors transformed him into a living symbol of what the church as a whole should be. Among those factors were: the intensity of his commitment to follow the path of the poor Jesus, his own religious genius, the action of the Holy Spirit, and the underlying spiritual needs of his era.

The voluntary poverty of Francis is the key: not poverty as symbol of helpless victimization but poverty as symbol both of the reigning idolatry as well as of the true Christian's solidarity with those whom idolatry victimizes. Francis became the living, walking embodiment both of the church's sin and of its necessary penance: the church's sin of allying itself with the grasping of power and possessions and the church's penance of allying itself with those who suffer from that idolatry. Francis dressed in the simplest of garments because that is the clothing (or lack of clothing) forced upon the poor.

"Forced" is the operative word. Francis understood that involuntary poverty is an act of violence. War is but that act writ large and glorified. At Damietta, he dressed and behaved as a symbol of contradiction to the prevailing idolatry.

If Francis Lived Today

Both Christians and Muslims might now ask themselves what Francis (or Jesus!) would be wearing if he were walking through America's cities and towns today. How would his bearing and clothing contradict current forms of idolatry? What *are* those forms, and what is the church doing about them? And what about the multiplying evidence of violence in contemporary American society, violence we perpetrate at home against each other and abroad in our ongoing wars in Muslim-dominant lands? What are we Christians prepared to do about them?

Or indeed, what are we *Muslims* prepared to do about them?

Because the point about Francis's behavior in embracing poverty is that his example applies just as much to Muslims as to Christians. It does not apply in quite the same way, or with the same meaning, but its relevance to Muslims is unmistakable. Muslims cannot accept Francis's own sense of identification with the risen Christ, but they do have many ways of understanding and admiring his ridding himself of horse, weapons, and fancy clothing for the sake of the poor. Muslims' appreciation of biblical social justice fundamentals — abhorrence of idolatry, covenant, solidarity with the poor — is just as strong as that of Christians or Jews. But Muslims can also appreciate the example of the poor, nonviolent Jesus, and therefore of Francis himself, as well as of the many other Christians since (including Mother Teresa of Calcutta) who strove to imitate him. The Sultan's own eagerness to dialogue with Francis reflects the longstanding Muslim tradition of venerating Christ not only as among the greatest of prophets but also as a wandering ascetic and champion of the poor.

Tarif Khalidi, in his *The Muslim Jesus,* has collected over three hundred sayings about Jesus culled from early Muslim tradition. All of them paint a picture of a figure, necessarily a completely human one, who could serve as Francis's twin. In one of these sayings, God is imagined addressing Jesus as follows:

> O Jesus, I have granted you love of the poor and mercy toward them. You love them, and they love you and accept you as their spiritual guide and leader, and you accept them as companions and followers. These are two traits of character. Know that whoever meets me on Judgment Day with these two character traits has met me with the purest of works and the ones most beloved by me.[21]

No wonder the Sultan was open to Francis's story. He may have thought that the great prophet, Jesus himself, had wandered into his tent!

Discussion Questions

1. What is the connection between Francis's radical companionship with the poor and his companionship with all of creation?

2. How do you understand the importance of the two most repeated themes of the Bible (idolatry and economic justice/poverty) in your life?

3. Is the notion of a "covenant community" only a nostalgic relic of the past? Where do you see expressions of it today?

4. How do you understand what Jesus was trying to say with the phrase "you always have the poor with you"?

5. If the Christian scriptures are "a consistent witness against violence" why are so few Christians committed to nonviolence?

Chapter 4

THE FUNDAMENTALS
OF ISLAMIC SOCIAL JUSTICE

The Sultan and Peacemaking

In chapter 3 we suggested that curiosity, rather than anxiety, marked the tone of the historic meeting between Francis and the Sultan. We suggested too that this curiosity wasn't idle. Rather, it proceeded from the men's deep confidence in their respective religious commitments. From that solid base they both found it natural to want to explore the mystery of God's relations with all God's creatures, not just with adherents of their own faiths.

It's important to clarify, however, that this openness was a very different thing from the modern phenomenon of relativism, a casual assumption that all religious beliefs are basically the same. Nor was it like the pluralism of today, where Muslims and Christians take advantage of the great strides taken by interfaith dialogue since the time of the Second Vatican Council to discuss their differences and commonalties peacefully and openly. No, back in 1219 it would not have been possible to escape a format of discussion that almost certainly would have resembled a spirited debate. One "side" would have presented its claims to truth; the other "side" would have done the same. But where in most cases Muslim-Christian debates of this type were tense and polemical, the debate between Francis and the Sultan, while lively, was nevertheless serene. The serenity is explicable only if we assume that both parties respected each other and were truly listening to each other. Their crucial and path-breaking mildness of tone had to do with the particular spiritual development of these two men, and, in particular, with the development in both of a predisposition to peacemaking.

We saw in the previous chapter how that predisposition grew strong in Francis. But what about the Sultan? Something in his prior experience must have led him, as it had led Francis, to see beyond the fears and prejudices of many of his fellow Muslims and to embrace a very different vision of how Muslims were to relate to the Other than through warfare and aggression. What was this "something"?

Unfortunately, we can't answer this question about the Sultan as confidently as we can about Francis, the reason being that we know so much more about the life of Francis than we do about the Sultan's. Besides that, the two men came from very different social spheres, so different, in fact, that their lives would have played out very differently even if they had been of the same religion. Francis's father was a clothing merchant. That's why, when Francis sold his expensive clothing back in Assisi, he was not only renouncing all luxury; he was also renouncing his ties with his father's social class and its values. Then, by undertaking a mendicant's lifestyle, he allied himself with society's castoffs, not with its lords and masters.

But lord and master was exactly who Sultan Malik al-Kamil was. In fact, the Arabic word *sultan* means "authority," and "Malik al-Kamil" means "The king is whole, nothing lacking." Far from breaking with his family's social class and values, as Francis did, Sultan Malik embodied them faithfully. Yet those values included what might seem a surprising element: a very strong emphasis on seeking peaceful solutions to conflicts, even to conflicts with the invading Crusaders.

How the Sultan Became "The Authority Is Whole"

Sultan Malik al-Kamil was a scion of a prominent Kurdish family forced south by dynastic change. Malik al-Kamil's grandfather, Ayyub, a member of this exiled family, rose to power first in Baghdad and then in Damascus, where he became governor. Ayyub carried on family tradition by exercising considerable diplomatic skills. One of his sons, the great Saladin, eventually became Sultan not only of Damascus but also of a vast domain stretching from Syria in the north to Yemen at the southern tip of the Arabian peninsula and from Palestine in the east to Baghdad in the west. Saladin, like his father Ayyub, was gifted both in diplomacy and war. In addition, he won lasting renown even among Christians for his chivalry. On October 2, 1187, after the Crusaders of the Second Crusade surrendered Jerusalem to Saladin's armies, Saladin ordered that Jerusalem's conquered Christian population be treated humanely, in contrast to the slaughter visited upon the city's then-Muslim inhabitants in 1099 by the Christian knights of the First Crusade.

Another son of Ayyub, al-Adil, Sultan Malik al-Kamil's father, played a key role as general and adviser to his brother Saladin in the battles leading up to the Crusaders' surrender of Jerusalem. Al-Adil continued to show his skills both as warrior and diplomat during the Third Crusade. After Richard the Lion-Hearted was unsuccessful in his attempt to retake Jerusalem in 1192, al-Adil negotiated with Richard to bring the opposing sides peacefully together through al-Adil's marriage to Richard's sister Joan. The marriage was never concluded, since Richard insisted on al-Adil's conversion to Christianity. A measure of concord was reached, however, when Richard conferred knighthood (a quasi-sacramental rite) on one of al-Adil's sons. That son was the eleven-year-old Malik al-Kamil. Ironically, Malik al-Kamil achieved early in life and without striking a blow the goal of knighthood that had been Francis's guiding light until his collapse after the battle at Perugia.

Al-Adil eventually became Sultan seven years after Saladin's death in 1193. He then appointed his three sons as viceroys over the Ayyub realm, with Malik al-Kamil receiving Egypt. Al-Adil taught all his sons to value discretion and finesse over violence in dealing with enemies. Malik al-Kamil throughout his career remained faithful to his father's teaching despite great pressure to do otherwise.

Malik's first great test came after the death of his father al-Adil, in 1218, just a year before Francis came to his tent. The Crusaders had made a feint of attacking Jerusalem. Sultan al-Adil had rushed to Damascus in the north to amass a counterattack. But the main body of the Crusaders had in mind a different goal: the capture of Egypt, which would not only give them a military advantage in an eventual assault on Jerusalem but would also open to them the vast riches of the Nile. Under the military leadership of John of Brienne, younger brother of the Walter of Brienne in whose armies Francis had once planned to gain glory, the Crusaders after a bloody battle captured the tower protecting the city of Damietta at the mouth of the Nile. Sultan al-Adil died of grief on hearing this news, leaving Malik al-Kamil, now Sultan of Egypt, with the responsibility of defending the city.

The Opposition of Pelagius

John of Brienne decided to wait for reinforcements before attacking the city. But John was overruled by a newcomer on the scene, Cardinal Pelagius Galvani, an Italian bishop to whom Pope Honorius had given the duty of crushing the Muslims in the Holy Land once and for all. Pelagius insisted that the Crusaders attack Damietta immediately. According to an eyewitness, Pelagius on one occasion before battle prayed "that we may be able to convert the perfidious and worthless people, so that they ought to believe with us in the Holy Trinity and in Your Nativity and in Your Passion and death and resurrection."[1]

Pelagius stands out as an antithesis of Francis. Francis wanted to convert the Sultan and other Muslims through peaceful persuasion and personal example; Pelagius through the sword.

As it turned out, the Crusaders were soon able to gain control of the ground near the fortified city of Damietta without fighting for it. Sultan Malik al-Kamil had to abandon his defense of the city in order to deal with a conspiracy against him that arose in the confusion after the death of his father, al-Adil. His manner of dealing with it shows the depth of his commitment to the Ayyub

tradition of peacemaking. Instead of annihilating the conspira-
tors, one of whom was Malik al-Kamil's younger brother, he sent
them off on various missions. Then he returned in haste to relieve
the besieged city. But the Crusaders had dug themselves in deeply
in the interval. The Sultan was not able to break the siege.

For a second time Malik al-Kamil showed his commitment to
peacemaking. Instead of sacrificing his soldiers' lives in a fanatical
and suicidal do-or-die last effort, and in the process risking the
lives of his subjects still within the city, the Sultan sued for peace,
offering the Crusaders their ostensible goal, Jerusalem, in return
for their leaving Egypt. But Pelagius proudly refused this offer,
not only on this occasion, but also on the many other occasions
during the next two years when Malik al-Kamil reoffered it to
him. Pelagius, under the pope's orders, insisted on the complete
subjugation of the Muslims. Nothing else would satisfy him.

By the time Francis arrived in Egypt in the summer of 1219,
the battle for control of Damietta had reached a bloody stalemate.
John of Brienne continued to argue that the Crusaders should
accept the Sultan's offers of peace, but Pelagius, who spoke in the
pope's name and controlled the army's funds as well, was always
able to overrule him. Pelagius's urging led to an all-out assault
on the Sultan's encampment, a decision Francis himself openly
opposed. (Many argue that Francis's opposition was directed not
just against this act of war, but against all acts of war everywhere.)
As Francis feared, the assault led to the rout of the Crusaders,
though it did not break their siege of the city. Characteristically,
the Sultan decided not to fall upon his enemy but to offer them
the same peace terms as before. Pelagius, however, remained firm.
The Crusaders had been bloodied but not driven away. Pelagius
turned down this latest of Sultan Malik al-Kamil's peace overtures,
confident that when reinforcements did arrive, he would be able
to crush the infidel.

Despairing of a change of heart on the part of Pelagius and
sickened by the scenes of slaughter around Damietta, which must
have reminded him of similar scenes at Perugia, Francis then

decided to take matters into his own hands. He went to Pelagius to ask permission to walk with his companion, Illuminato, through enemy lines to see if peace could be achieved through the Sultan's conversion. Reluctantly Pelagius gave his permission. He washed his hands of the consequences, saying: "All this is to be your sole responsibility, because certainly I shall not be the one to send you to your certain death."[2]

As we know, Sultan Malik al-Kamil did not live up to the typecasting of Pelagius. He did not kill Francis on sight but treated him graciously, even after a year of devastating attacks upon the Sultan and his people and his religion by the Christian invaders. We know already one cause of his preference for peace: fidelity to the teaching and example of his Ayyub forebears. But what was the basis of this fidelity? Filial loyalty alone? Or a rational assessment of diplomacy's tactical value in situations where one's forces don't have an overwhelming advantage, as was certainly Sultan Malik al-Kamil's situation at Damietta? We don't have to deny such influences in order to emphasize their deepest grounding in Islam itself. Sultan al-Malik, a man thoroughly conversant with and attentive to his religion's teachings and values, knew that peacemaking is at the heart of the Qur'an's revelations. Whatever he imbibed from his family's practice of diplomacy and whatever he discovered through reason were secondary to the Qur'an's central teaching, in a phrase we discussed in chapter 1, "There is no god but God," the first half of the Muslim *shahadah*.

To see how that is so, we need to understand this teaching as fully as possible in its theological and ethical dimensions. And then we need to see how the teaching predisposed Sultan Malik al-Kamil toward peacemaking both on the battlefield and in his tent with the Sufi-like figure come to convert him to the religion of the "enemy."

The Muslim Social Justice Tradition

The Qur'anic line "There is no god but God," in Arabic *la ilha illa Allah,* asserts, as we know, *tauhid,* the unicity of God. And because God is One, God's creation is fundamentally one as well, since all created things owe their existence to one and one source only. From this belief in God's oneness and in the fundamental unity of creation flows a religious attitude on humankind's part of self-surrender to God (*islam,* in the word's root sense — see chapter 1) and an ethical disposition toward solidarity with God's creation. Solidarity is achieved by peacemaking, not through war.

It is no accident, then, that just as the biblical tradition connects God's warnings against idolatry and God's urgent appeal for concern for the poor, the Muslim tradition does the same. In fact, in the Muslim tradition, idolatry, *shirk,* as an offense both against God and against solidarity with God's creation, is even more explicitly condemned than it is in the New Testament. This greater emphasis has to do with a point made earlier, that Islam, while drawing its inspiration from the same prophetic tradition from which Judaism and Christianity grew, emerged out of a polytheistic context. Idol worship was the dominant form of religion of the tribes to whom Prophet Muhammad brought God's revelations. Idolatry's failure to conceive of a life after death and of moral values transcending those associated with ensuring the individual tribe's survival became major targets of the Qur'an's attack. Alternatively, love and worship of the One God and service to the one humanity created by God became the objects of the Qur'an's constant appeal.

Covenant in Islam

That appeal by God to humankind results in covenant (*mithaq,* in Arabic) just as it does in the biblical scriptures. But whereas the Bible, as we saw in chapter 3, speaks of at least four covenants: with Noah after the flood, with Abraham and Sarah, with Moses and the Hebrews in the desert at Mt. Sinai, and with Jesus and his disciples (for Christians, the covenant that supersedes all others), the Qur'an speaks of only one, a primordial covenant humankind made with God before the dawning of humankind's history.

The account of this covenant is given in Sura al-A'raf 7:172–74:

When your Cherisher and Sustainer drew from their seed all the descendants of the children of Adam so that they might give witness about themselves and when we asked them, "Am I not your Cherisher and Sustainer?" they all answered, "Yes, we witness that you are." This was done so that none of you could say at the Day of Judgment, "We were never aware of this!" And so that none of you could say, "Our ancestors were the ones who were idolaters. We belong to a later generation. Can you really intend to destroy us because of what those fools did?"

The point of the parable is to say that all human beings without exception have made the fundamental choice to enter into covenant with God. They did so by answering, "Yes" to God's "Am I not your Cherisher and Sustainer?" There was never a time when humankind did not enter into this covenant, because humankind gave its free assent when humankind was in "seed," that is, before human history began. The history following humankind's primordial assent is where the trouble begins, because it is in the unfolding of history that humankind finds ways of forgetting or disfiguring its original witness. So whereas humankind exercised God's gift of free will properly at its creation, by using it in *islam* (self-surrender) to God, humankind tended to pervert or "cover over" the gift as the generations emerged from their seed. They took the gift itself while forgetting or denying the giver. ("Cover over" is the root meaning from which the Qur'anic term *kafir*, "infidel," is derived; an "infidel" is one who "covers over" a gift so that one can claim it as one's own creation and possession.)

The purpose of prophecy is to remind humankind of its commitment to the primordial covenant. For this reason the Qur'an says it is not bringing anything new into the world but that it is instead restating in an especially clear way the truth to which humankind originally assented. The Qur'an is truly an "old" testament. It is in its own words nothing more or less than a *zikr*, "a reminder."

Centered in Creation

Where the Christian social justice tradition is primarily centered on the new covenant between the risen Christ and sinful humanity, the Muslim social justice tradition is primarily centered on the original covenant between God and humanity during the moment of humanity's creation and before the entry of humankind into history. But for all its attention to the primordial conditions of this moment, the Qur'an teaches that God's creative activity extends beyond those conditions and in fact that it is continuous, constantly renewing and sustaining the creation it has brought into being. Yet God's creative activity is purposive as well. God is not simply perpetuating a given set of conditions. God is seeking to bring these conditions to perfection. So while the created world is rooted in the past, it is constantly unfolding toward its eventual completion in the world and in the life to come.

The logic of Islam's "creational covenant" can be seen in six linked propositions. The first proposition is that God's freedom as creator is absolute. The phrase that introduces all 114 suras of the Qur'an but one emphasizes this absoluteness. The phrase is, "In the name of God, the Most Beneficent, the Most Merciful," a phrase we encountered in chapter 2 at the beginning of the first sura of the Qur'an, called the *Fatihah* or Opening. After God's name (Allah) comes a second name, *ar-rahman,* translated here "the Most Beneficent." This Arabic name *ar-rahman* is used only for God because it denotes the unique freedom of God's creative act. In no way was God compelled to create the world. No external necessity or "law" of any kind drove God to be beneficent in this unfathomably profound way.

A second proposition follows from the first. Having been so beneficent as to bring the world into being in the first place, God continues to bring it into being at every moment. According to the Qur'an, there is no Sabbath. God creates the world in six days, then mounts His "throne" to maintain it. As the Qur'an puts it in Sura al-Baqarah 2:255, "He neither sleeps nor does He slumber," but is at every instant actively present to each element of creation, from the gnat to the mountain range to the galaxy, saying to each thing, "Be!" and again "Be!" and again "Be!"

The third proposition is that while God's created universe is splendid in its variety, it is organized and directed by the principle of *tauhid,* or unicity. Unicity follows, as we have seen, from the fact that God is One. There cannot be multiple creators or even a "principle" or "law" of creation or even a law of God's own nature to which God is subject (with one exception — see proposition six, below). On a more pragmatic level, there cannot be a human creative agency that in any way rivals the creativity that is God's and God's alone. Accordingly humankind cannot arrogate greater or even similar powers of creativity to itself, whether those powers are artistic, political, or of any other kind. Nor can humankind treat others as if they could possess such power (for example, worshiping a mortal like Jesus/'Isa as if he were God). Nor can human beings worship their own egos or desires or obsessions in this way.

Proposition four entails that God's creatures respond to God's unicity, or *tauhid,* through *islam,* self-surrender. *Islam* in its broadest dimension refers to all God's creatures, not just to human beings. *Islam* refers to the way all created things faithfully obey the natures God has created for them and by this means render God praise. The gnat and the mountain range and the galaxy, different as they are from each other, are unified by their mutual dedication to being faithfully what God intends them to be: a gnat, a mountain range, a galaxy. The gnat does not strive to be a mountain range, nor the mountain range a gnat. In this way, through their faithfulness to their created natures, they each manifest their ultimate unity. The Qur'an calls all such created things *muslim,* another form of the word *islam.* (Grammatically, *islam* is the noun for self-surrender and *muslim* is the participle used as noun, indicating the one who self-surrenders.) And because all things are *muslim* in relation to God, they are "just" in relation to each other. No created thing ever attempts to usurp the being of another, claim it as his own, in an effort to become what God did not intend it to be.

No created thing? Alas, there is one exception, humankind itself. This is the fifth proposition. Like all other created things, humankind has been given a certain nature, but this human nature is more problematic than the nature given other created beings because humankind has been uniquely endowed with God's *ruh,* or spirit. *Ruh,* or spirit, is usually identified in this case with free will, with a fragment, that is, of God's own creative freedom of spirit. This special endowment of free will means that humankind's *islam,* self-surrender, is constantly in doubt. Unlike all other creatures, humankind tends to resist surrendering itself in praise to God. Forgetting its original witness while in the seed of Adam, humankind wants to keep itself all to itself, so to speak.

Humankind even wants to make itself into a god so that it can worship that self! This fundamental distortion of *islam* results in the hideous distortion of humankind's own nature, like a gnat pretending it is truly a galaxy. And this distortion, what the Qur'an labels a fundamental injustice to the self, results in all manner of distortions of people's relationships with each other and with all other creatures. It is the cause of all violence (in Arabic, *jahiliya,* a state of frantic, self-destructive ignorance).

We come now to the sixth and last proposition in this list of consequences flowing from the beneficence of God. Looking again at the beginning of the *Fatihah,* or Opening, we see, after *ar-rahman,* a third name for God, *ar-rahim,* translated here "the Most Merciful." This Arabic name, *ar-rahim,* is used not only for God but for people, because this is the word for what brings God to intervene in God's own creation on our behalf. *Ar-rahman* and *ar-rahim* together express the full range of God's solicitude for His creation, from the incomprehensible loftiness of God's original and sustaining "Be!" to God's unfailing offer of intimacy and guidance to every part of that creation, even (or most especially) to the most errant part of it, humankind. So central is Beneficence and Mercy to God's relation to creation that "He has inscribed Mercy upon himself as a law" (Sura An'am 6:12). As the great Muslim scholar Fazlur Rahman puts it:

God exercises His greatness, power, and all-comprehensive presence primarily through the entire range of the manifestations of mercy — through being and creation, sustenance of that creation, guiding that creation to its destiny, and, finally, through a "return" to the creatures who, after willful alienation, sincerely wish to be reconciled to the source of their being, life, and guidance.[3]

Like a concerned mother (both *ar-rahman* and *ar-rahim* are derived from the word for "womb"), God uses the Qur'an itself to shake humanity free of its distractedness and ego worship and injustice to itself and to others and to bring it back to what the *Fatihah* calls the "straight path" — to bring humanity back to *islam,* for from *islam* flows right relations with God and with each other.

The Qur'an's Intersection with Human History

The Qur'an is not a treatise on abstract themes any more than the Bible is. Like the Bible (whose basic message of loving God and serving the neighbor the Qur'an honors as an authentic "reminder" handed down to their people by the prophet Moses and by the prophet Jesus) the Qur'an is a revelation, the sign of God's engagement in humankind's history. The Qur'an itself is a compilation of revelations that came down to the prophet Muhammad over a twenty-two-year period from 610. (beginning when the Prophet was forty years old) to his death in 632. The revelations are not bloodless statements from a source detached from human struggle. They are utterances directly addressed to what Muslims call "occasions" (*asbab*), particular crises in the lives of the people to whom they are directed. The first of those people is the Prophet Muhammad himself. Many of the Qur'an's utterances are addressed specifically to him, giving him advice and encouraging him. Yet the Prophet Muhammad is never singled out as the sole recipient of the utterances. He is always their "messenger" to a people grievously in need of hearing them.

We hinted above at the source of that need: the fracturing of human community brought about by idolatry. The Qur'an both reveals the fracturing and provides the way to heal it.

The revelations that were sent down to the Prophet Muhammad during the first period of his prophetic career, at Mecca, sought to wake the people of that caravan crossroads and pilgrimage town to the depth of their spiritual peril. They had long forgotten their creational covenant with the One God. In addition, Mecca's ruling tribe, the Quraysh, had become rich from taxing caravan traffic, and because of its newfound wealth and prestige had forgotten the rudimentary ethic of solidarity and support for the weakest within its own tribal group. The division between the haves and have-nots increased. Lacking belief in life after death and final judgment, the leaders of the Quraysh worshiped whichever god rewarded them with material success. They feared no consequences for greed and abuse of power.

The Qur'an "reminded" the Quraysh of their covenantal promises to the One God and warned them of the consequences of persisting to "forget" them: eventual calamity in this life and eternal damnation in the next. Not surprisingly such a reminder and such a warning aroused hatred for their messenger, just as it did for similar messages brought by biblical prophets and by Jesus. Even in such a hostile climate Muhammad was able to gather many followers during the twelve years of his proclamation of the Qur'an in Mecca, though the majority of these were socially disadvantaged. Among them were women, slaves, and members of lesser clans of the Quraysh, like his own. But by 622, Muhammad and his community were forced by increasing threats to life and limb on the part of the Quraysh leadership to abandon Mecca and to reestablish themselves in a town to the north called Yathrib.

It was here in Yathrib, soon renamed Medina (the short form of *Medinat an-Nabi,* "City of the Prophet"), where the second part of Muhammad's career began. Key tribes in Medina welcomed the Prophet and encouraged him to try to unite their fragmented polity. No longer the persecuted prophet, Muhammad took on new roles as occasion demanded: lawgiver to the young Muslim community as well as its defender in battle. For the young community almost immediately was forced to ward off attack by Meccans as well as by surrounding tribes. These smaller tribes were as unwilling as the Quraysh were to submit to a common moral code based upon the fundamental unity of all humankind. All saw the new Muslim community, not only as an existential threat to their privileged way of life, but now as a physical threat as well.

The revelations of the Medina period reflect the change in Muhammad's fortunes. While the Meccan emphasis on the fundamentals of covenant faith remains, the Medinan revelations often deal with particular crises of leadership Muhammad encountered as he attempted, ultimately successfully, to shape the moral and political ethos of the new community and to establish its security. Central to the first of these endeavors was a series of revelations that insisted on fairness toward classes of people previously marginalized either by tribal ethic or by the rapaciousness of the Quraysh: toward women, female infants (often exposed in the desert if deemed to be "unnecessary"), widows, orphans, those who were poor, wayfarers. Central to the second of these endeavors was the Qur'an's encouragement of *jihad*.

Jihad *as the Basis of Peacemaking*

Jihad is among all Qur'anic concepts the least understood. It is treated in the Western media as denoting a supposedly divine sanction of violence. Yet *jihad* (Arabic for "striving for a good end") is actually the very opposite of that; *jihad,* in one of its two meanings, is the divine sanctioning of a "just war" approach to intergroup conflict. As the Qur'an teaches it, *jihad* allows Muslims to retaliate against enemies, but never to be the aggressors. If attacked, Muslims must assure the safety of noncombatants and must cease hostilities as soon as the attacks against them cease. Finally, *jihad* obliges Muslims to offer terms of peace to their enemies as soon as possible.

Those who seek to prove that *jihad* gives a simple license to kill "prove" their point by selective quoting of the Qur'an ("cherry-picking"). But full quoting of Qur'anic verses where *jihad* is encouraged reveals the many ways in which the conduct of warfare is hedged about with restrictions, all with the view of reaching peaceful resolution of conflict.

Here are the first sixteen verses of Sura at-Tauba as an example:

9:1A treaty of immunity from God and his messenger Muhammad to those among the pagan Bedouin tribes with whom you have made alliances: 9:2Go anywhere you want throughout the earth, you idolaters [i.e., pagan Bedouin tribes], for four months, but be aware that God will not be fooled by your treachery. Rather, God will bring shame on those who deny him.

9:3And an announcement from God and his messenger to the people gathered on the day of the Great Hajj to Mecca: that God is freed of all connection with idolaters at Mecca itself — and his messenger is freed as well. Even then, you idolaters, if you turn in repentance to God, it will be best for you. But if you turn away, be aware that you cannot fool God. So announce to those who deny God a terrible consequence.

9:4All this shall happen except to those idolaters with whom you have made alliances and who since then have never betrayed you in any way, nor given aid behind your back to enemies. 9:5But when the four months are over and the other party has persisted in its treachery, then fight the idolaters wherever you find them. Seize them, beset them, besiege them, wait for them in ambush. Yet still — if they repent, if they observe daily prayer, if they give to the poor, then clear the way for them. Remember that God is all-forgiving, most merciful.

9:6And if one of the idolaters seeks you out for protection, then grant it to him, so that he may hear the word of God.

Afterward, escort him to a safe place. Such things happen because they are a people without knowledge of God.

9:7How can there be an alliance with idolaters in God's sight and in the sight of the messenger, except for those with whom you made alliances near the Sacred Mosque in Mecca? As long as they stand firm in their commitment to you, do the same with them. Remember that God loves those who are attentive to him and him alone.

9:8But again, how can there be an alliance with idolaters since, if they get the better of you in some way, they respect neither kinship ties nor treaties? They please you with their mouths, uttering friendly phrases, but in their hearts they scorn you. The greater part of them are transgressors, they know no bounds. 9:9They have sold God's words for a trifle and have hindered others from God's way. Their deeds are in every way evil. 9:10They do not respect kinship ties with a believer — nor treaties either. Clearly it is they who have transgressed all bounds.

9:11Yet — if they repent, if they keep regular prayers, if they give alms, then they shall become your brothers in worship. This is how we explain our signs to a people who understand.

9:12But if they violate their trust after they make their treaties with you, if they mock you for your faithfulness, then fight those great exemplars of faithlessness! Their word means nothing to them. So fight them — perhaps they will learn to restrain themselves.

9:13Will you not fight a people who has violated its trust? Who are plotting even now to expel the messenger from Medina? Didn't they attack you first? What? Are you afraid of them? Yet it is more reasonable to fear God if you are true believers.

9:14So, fight them! Using your hands, God will punish them, he will cover them with shame, he will help you overcome them. And God will heal believers' hearts of all injury caused by violence. 9:15For he will remove their fury and give them peace. God turns in mercy to whomever he pleases. Remember that God is all-knowing, all-wise.

9:16Or did you hope that you would be let alone? That God would not test you to learn who among you practices *Jihad*? to learn who among you counts no one his intimate friend but God and his messenger and the other believers? Remember that God is very much aware of everything you do.

The connection between *jihad* and God's creational covenant with humankind follows from the unity of humankind. When humankind was called forth from the seed of Adam, it was called forth as a body of equals. The one and only distinction imputed to individual members of humankind was each person's will to remain faithful to his or her response to God's, "Am I not your Cherisher and Sustainer?" As human lives unfold in history, the character of the individual will reveal itself in private as well as in communal behavior. Choices made that turn other people into objects (as less than equal in humanity with oneself) are signs of defiance of the primordial covenant. Injustice to others is injustice to oneself and vice versa. As the Qur'an asserts in Sura al-Ma'idah 5:35: "Whoever kills another human being (unless the person is guilty of murder or corruption) — it is as if he killed all humankind; whoever saves a life — it is as if he saved all humankind."

What *jihad* provides for, then, in the passage above and everywhere else in the Qur'an, is a way to resolve conflicts with fellow human beings who have chosen to differ from their brothers and sisters on the basis of the one point that *does* separate them: not their tribal allegiances or their social status or their skin color or their language or even their religion but their fidelity to their creational covenant. That is why in the verses above the Qur'an constantly urges the faithful to hold off from battle as soon as the unfaithful (the old word for this in English is "infidel") relent and return to the covenant. Warfare begins as the young Muslim community's act of self-protection; but its real goal is the conversion of heart of those who have hardened it against their common humanity and against the God from whom that common human bond derives.

We said above that one of the meanings of *jihad* advocates a "just war" approach to intergroup conflict. The second meaning, actually the deeper one, connects communal behavior under siege to individual moral discipline and spirituality. *Jihad,* in this second and more fundamental sense, involves the active disposition of the whole person toward what can be called "inner peacemaking." A well-documented *hadith* gives the Prophet's own sense of *jihad*'s layered meanings. During the Medina period a group of war- riors returned to Muhammad's camp after a successful skirmish with Meccan attackers. The Prophet said to them, "You have been engaged in the Lesser *Jihad*. The Greater *Jihad* is the battle to gain control over your mind and heart." The Greater *Jihad* precedes the Lesser. Righteous communal behavior, whether in warfare, in business, in law, or in any other activity, cannot be sustained if it does not originate in a purification of the individual's will. Yet purification requires effort. Human beings who overcome their obsessions (with power, self, wealth, prestige, to name a few of the idols with which people torment themselves and others) pay a price. But the reward is the vista opening up to them in inner peace, in harmonious relations with others, and in closeness with God, not to mention in the joy and fulfillment of the life to come.

Jihad *and Sultan Malik al-Kamil*

Our Muslim sources don't say specifically how *jihad* shaped Sultan Malik al-Kamil's behavior. That's not surprising. *Jihad* is such a fundamental concept in Islam that a Muslim's adhering to it would be assumed. But for our purposes it's interesting to use the passage from Sura at-Tauba above as a guide to the Sultan's behavior during the stress of the Crusaders' assault.

We have to remember, however, that the passage from Sura at-Tauba addresses a particular set of situations faced by Prophet Muhammad's community. The Muslims' enemies then were treach- erous Bedouin tribes and Meccans. The Sultan, centuries later, found himself facing a quite different enemy, not self-confessed idolators this time, but Christians, whom the Qur'an calls "People of the Message," that is, a community who also worshiped the One God (though with the painful difference — as we've already noted — that Christians "associated" God with a man, Jesus or 'Isa). The Crusaders had not broken any specific peace treaty. In fact, the challenge for Sultan Malik al-Kamil was to induce them to enter into such a treaty. Yet the Crusaders, by virtue of the scale and violence of their assaults on Muslims since the First Crusade, had become a formidable threat to the Muslim world, its culture, and its religion. The community must be defended. *Jihad* must be evoked.

What is striking about the Sultan's behavior toward the Crusaders is how consistently it displays the essentially defensive nature of the Lesser *Jihad*. And we have looked only at his behavior in the first year of this conflict. We will see later that this consistency characterized his behavior right through to the end of the Fifth Crusade — and beyond. But not only in his relation to the Crusader army does the Sultan display defensive restraint. His behavior to Francis seems almost dictated by a particular verse of Sura at-Tauba (9:6): "And if one of the idolaters seeks you out for protection, then grant it to him, so that he may hear the word of God. Afterward, escort him to a safe place. Such things happen because they are a people without knowledge of God."

The Sultan would not have regarded Francis as an "idolater." Still, just as Francis felt compelled to preach Christianity to the Sultan, the Sultan, for his part, probably felt compelled to preach "knowledge of God" in his turn. But in no case could he use physical force on one who sought his "protection." And no force was to be used to convert his guest, since the Qur'an explicitly says: "No compulsion in religion" (Sura al-Baqarah 2:256). Then, afterward, the Christian Sufi, Francis, was to be "escorted to a safe place."

Is that all? Just a display of exemplary Muslim manners on the Sultan's part? Given the circumstances, such a display would have been a lot to ask of Malik al-Kamil. Yet the Sultan seems to have gone much further. Perhaps he invited Francis to participate with him in the Lesser *Jihad:*

> 9:14And God will heal believers' hearts of all injury caused by violence. 9:15For he will remove their fury and give them peace. (Sura at-Tauba)

It is hard not to believe that such a verse echoed in the Sultan's memory as he listened to Francis speak to him about Christ's love for all creatures. It is hard not to believe that he recited this line in reply and that both men experienced together a healing of hearts.

If the Sultan Lived Today

At the end of chapter 3, we wondered what Francis would be doing and thinking if he were walking through America's cities and towns today. How would his living witness to radical poverty resonate in our contemporary world? Would he be arrested for vagrancy? Or would he renew in us a sense of deep contrition for the violence and greed that still dominate our culture? Would he inspire us to nonviolent challenges to those behaviors?

We can wonder also about what the Sultan would be doing or thinking if he were with us today. As an embodiment of the Muslim virtue of *jihad,* the Sultan sets a standard against which the behavior of contemporary Muslim extremists can be judged. Osama bin Laden's callousness with regard to the lives of innocent victims is a travesty of *jihad* as the Qur'an enjoins it and as the Sultan practiced it. But it is not only today's Muslim *jihad*ists who should be condemned by the Sultan's standards. Generals and presidents calling themselves Christians bear the responsibility for an aggressive (euphemistically dubbed "pre-emptive") war in Iraq, which by some estimates has caused the death, injury, and displacement of hundreds of thousands of noncombatants.

On an even deeper level, many of today's Muslims and Christians come up short when measured against the Sultan's fidelity to our primordial covenant. Muslims come up short whenever they talk and act as if the covenant embraces only Muslims, or just Muslims of their own sectarian or political persuasion. Christians come up short when they forget that Muslims too participate in the primordial covenant. Christians do believe that God created the world and humankind to be "good." But some Christians have tended to lose a creational perspective (as well as a prophetic perspective derived from God's covenants with Israel) in order to stress the distinctiveness of Christian salvation and the vision of social justice that flows from salvation. But by opening themselves to Islam's emphasis on God's sanctifying of creation, as Notre Dame theologian Father David Burrell urges in his *Freedom and Creation in Three Traditions,* Christians can restore a balance between their honoring of creation and salvation. Such balance is necessary to prevent Christians from falling into a narrow sectarianism, one that would lead them to believe that created reality outside the Christian dispensation somehow does not belong to God.

Francis and the Sultan, if among us today, might agree they have more in common with each other than with many members of their own religions. Both obeyed, in their different ways, God's call to solidarity with all humankind, not just to preferred parts of it. *La ilaha illa Allah,* there is no god but God, is a credo both could assert, if not in the same words, then in their actions and lives.

Discussion Questions

1. How could it happen that Sultan Malik al-Kamil, a Muslim, was able to achieve what Francis, a Christian, never achieved — knighthood?

2. What prevented Sultan Malik from killing Francis on sight?

3. The Qur'an speaks of a primordial covenant. How does this covenant compare to the covenants in the Hebrew and Christian scriptures?

4. An "infidel" (*kafir*) is one who "covers over" a gift and denies the giver. Explain why this concern is so central in Islamic thought. Is there a similar concern in Christianity?

5. Explain the various meanings of *jihad*. Does Christianity have a parallel concept?

Part III

Greeting the Angels
(as Well as Confronting the Demons)
of Our Historical Relationship

Chapter 5

THE BLESSINGS OF OUR RELIGIOUS AND CULTURAL SHARING

The Openness of Francis

Francis's openness toward Muslims took shape within the crusading ideology of his day and to some degree reflected that ideology. Muslims were for both Francis and Pope Innocent III the Enemy Other. Both men started from the same place, the negative image of Islam prevalent in the countries of the West. This image was shaped by fear, envy, and ignorance: fear of Muslim military prowess, envy of Muslim cultural superiority, and ignorance of the religion and its people. For their part, neither the pope nor Francis (at least until he met the Sultan himself at Damietta) seems to have had any personal experience with Muslims that might have softened or at least complicated their simplistic image of them.

Yet Francis and the pope reacted very differently on the basis of that hostile characterization, with the pope declaring Holy War and Francis citing Christ's law of love. In that respect Francis's openness to Sultan Malik al-Kamil at Damietta marked the fulfillment of a hope that had guided Francis for years. This hope was that he could some day put fully in practice Jesus' command to "love your enemy." Of course Francis had been putting the command into practice ever since his conversion to what we now term Christian nonviolence after the battle of Perugia. But obeying the command of Jesus went beyond achieving a private spiritual goal.

It entailed instilling the command of Jesus in others, especially in those of his countrymen at each other's throats.

Since violence was the order of the day, Francis repeatedly found himself obliged to intervene in hostile situations in order to bring peace. He preached against war between the nobles and merchants of his old enemy, Perugia. He warned the warring factions of Arezzo that their violence shackled them, as he put it, "in demons' chains."[1] He intervened successfully in strife-torn Siena and Bologna. The legendary account of Francis's taming the wolf of Gubbio can be read as an allegory of his power as peacemaker. Increasingly, Francis saw greed and pride at the root of warfare. Because of that, poverty became for him an ever more potent symbol of peacemaking, of freedom from the ego-drives that make violence inevitable.

Preaching the love of enemies by word and example within his own Christian world was ambitious enough. But in the climate of his time Muslims were the Enemy par excellence. Bringing the Gospel of peace to them would be the greatest test of fidelity to Christ.

Francis made two efforts prior to his voyage to Egypt to establish nonviolent contact with Muslims. His first attempt occurred in 1211, when he took a ship for the Holy Land. But he had to abandon the attempt after the ship was blown off course. In 1213 or 1214 another opportunity to reach out to Muslims presented itself, not in the Holy Land, however, but in Morocco at the court of the Almohad emir Muhammad an-Nasir. Francis followed the legendary path of the apostle James across northern Spain to James's shrine at Compostela. From there he hoped to head south. He got no farther, however, probably because of illness. He managed to return to Rome in time for the opening of the Fourth Lateran Council. It was here that Pope Innocent III promulgated the Fifth Crusade on November 30, 1215, even though Sultan Malik al-Adil (Sultan Malik al-Kamil's father) had just entered into a five-year truce with the Latin kingdom of Palestine (a remnant of the crusading kingdom established after the First Crusade).

Francis wanted his young order of friars to support the church's effort to bring the Gospel to nonbelievers and especially to Muslims. He knew this could not be done without the pope's support. But at the same time his deep commitment to the nonviolent Christ made it impossible for him to preach the Crusade. Francis's idea was always to offer the Gospel of peace to the church's enemies, not the sword. Accordingly, he and his friars were to make their way to their Muslim enemies unescorted by armies.

Church authorities eager to support Francis were nervous, however, about this radical divergence from the pope's crusading ideology. So they sought to recast Francis's apparently suicidal idea of mission into a deliberate seeking of martyrdom. Such a motive was pleasing to those promoting the Fifth Crusade. Martyrdom had played a key part in the spread of the Christian faith during Roman rule; contemporary martyrdom at the hands of Muslims would draw on Christians' historic veneration of martyrs while confirming belief in Muslim bloodthirstiness. Martyrdom could in this way help inflame the ardor of the Crusaders. But while Francis always said that he and his friars must be prepared for death, he said also that they must not deliberately seek it. Their purpose was to act according to the law of love they preached, not to provoke the enemy into murder.

The Openness of Sultan Malik al-Kamil

Sultan Malik al-Kamil had plenty of reasons, especially after the crusading armies landed at Damietta, to see Christians as they saw him, as the Enemy Other. But his attitude toward the Crusaders was much more complex than the Crusaders' attitude was toward him. He had lived among Christians all his life. He had even been knighted by Christians, as we mentioned in chapter 4. And in Egypt he had a large population of Coptic Christians under his jurisdiction, first in his role as viceroy under his father, al-Adil, and then, after al-Adil's death, as Sultan.

By all accounts, including contemporary Christian ones, Sultan Malik's attitude toward the Christians over whom he ruled was a tolerant one, even more tolerant than his father's had been. Egyptian Christians told of the Sultan's leniency with Christian converts to Islam who later decided to revert to Christianity — the sort of decision punished by some Muslim rulers with death. Stories were also told of the Sultan's fair judgments in property conflicts between Muslim and Christian claimants. The Sultan intervened judiciously in Christian disputes about the appointment of the Coptic patriarch. He sought trade pacts with Venice and other Italian cities. In 1215, the year in which the pope proclaimed the Fifth Crusade, three thousand Christian merchants were living safely in Egypt.[2] And finally, as we saw in chapter 1, the Sultan had great interest in and fondness for Christian monks. Nor was Francis the first monk the Sultan had befriended. The Sultan had even asked one of those monks to pray for him during an illness.

The History of Muslim-Christian Relations: The Positive Side

Francis and the Sultan stand out during their time as lonely examples of the blessings of religious and cultural sharing. On the basis of their story alone we might draw the conclusion that the fruitfulness of their encounter was an anomaly, a singular, unrepeated, and unrepeatable event, perhaps even a miracle. Yet a broader perspective reveals that Muslims and Christians had already enjoyed a long history of positive if complex interchange. Knowing this history gives us hope that the angels we can imagine hovering protectively over the Sultan's tent in 1219 will strengthen today's Muslims and Christians and guide them in interfaith peacemaking. We can look to the historical record, not just to Damietta alone, as the source of confidence that past acts of Muslim and Christian solidarity can be used to support similar and even greater efforts in the present and in the future.

Historical records are always mixed, however. In the next chapter we'll take up the story that has dominated the narrative of Muslim-Christian relations over the centuries and that continues to overshadow it, the negative story, the sad tale of rivalry, violence, and recrimination between the two religions and the cultures that formed around them. There is, unfortunately, much evidence to support this dark account. But it needs to be balanced by the ongoing story of how Christians and Muslims have at their best not only learned from each other but have also worked together for the common good.

The Challenges of Scripture as History

Before we look at the historical record, though, we should review what the Qur'an and the New Testament have to say or imply about the possibilities of Muslim-Christian solidarity. We do so conscious that the two scriptures are themselves in a certain sense part of the historical record. We say this with no disrespect to the claims of Christians that the writing of New Testament was inspired by the Holy Spirit or to the claims of Muslims that the Qur'an is the exact record of God's words as given through the angel Gabriel to the Prophet Muhammad. For the fact is that both scriptures are revelations: they are in their different ways interventions on God's part into human history. They do not stand apart from human history in a timeless realm of philosophical abstraction but instead manifest God's ongoing concern to guide human beings in their struggles and confusions here and now.

One fact about the New Testament bears out its historical nature with respect to Islam: this fact is that the New Testament does not mention Islam or Muslims at all, for the simple reason that the last of the texts included in the New Testament were written four centuries before Prophet Muhammad received the first verse of what became the Qur'an. Accordingly, the New Testament has nothing whatever to say about Islam. The Qur'an, however, has much to say about Christianity and Christians. This follows from the fact that Christians were a part of Muhammad's world.

The asymmetry of reference caused by the temporal priority of the Christian scriptures means that in formulating our attitudes toward Islam, Christians have to work by inference. We have to interpret their experience with Muslims in the light of what the New Testament says about how Christians should treat those of other faiths.

For Muslims the interpretive challenge of dealing with Christians is in a sense easier, just because the Qur'an says so much about them. For Muslims, an understanding of Christianity and Christians is an explicit part of revelation, as it can never be for Christians. God has given Muslims direct guidance in their exchanges with Christians. Christians have no such direct guidance in their exchanges with Muslims.

Yet if Muslims enjoy an advantage in this respect, they also suffer a consequence: direct scriptural guidance can become a liability given the fact that the historical situation shaping both Muslims and Christians has changed greatly since Muhammad's day. The Qur'an's pronouncements on Christians are in answer to the particular experiences of Muhammad and his young community with them in the Arabian peninsula during the first three decades of the seventh century. A too literal interpretation of those pronouncements by Muslims of later eras, including our own, can lead to serious misunderstandings. Yet broader interpretation is risky since the Qur'an by its nature is God's very word.

Christians can be said, by contrast, to enjoy greater interpretive freedom in understanding Islam since their New Testament is silent on the subject. Yet this freedom brings with it the drawback that it can easily be abused. There is no explicit prohibition on Christians' seeing Muslims in the New Testament's most negative categories: as agents of Satan or as minions of the Anti-Christ, for example.

The truth is that neither Muslims nor Christians are absolved of the obligation of interpretation. Both must understand their respective revelations in the context of the present moment. To do this requires great patience and self-understanding. But patience and self-understanding must be based on knowledge of each religion's past relationships with each other, beginning with the scriptural record.

What the Qur'an Says about Christians and Christianity

Professor Sydney Griffiths characterizes the Qur'an's attitude toward Christians as "rather ambiguous." [3] What Professor Griffiths means is that the Qur'an at some points finds much to praise about Christians and Christianity and at others much to criticize. Take the example of the Qur'an's attitude toward monks. In chapter 1 we quoted a Qur'anic verse that calls Christians "nearest in love to Muslim believers . . . because among them are . . . monks, for these never puff themselves up." In other verses, however, monks are criticized for hoarding wealth in their monasteries (Sura at-Tauba 9:34) and for their "innovation" of ascetic celibacy (Sura al-Hadid 57:27). Disparities like these can be explained in part by differences in the historical experience to which the Qur'an is responding.

That experience became more complex and troubled as time went on. During the early period of Muhammad's preaching, in Mecca, the Qur'an tended to speak warmly of Christians. Local Christians seem to have responded to Muhammad far more positively than did Muhammad's own tribe, the Quraysh. And why should they not? The revelations coming to Muhammad were not innovations. They were affirmations of the divine mandate that Christians had already received through the prophet Jesus. Since God was One, God's revelation was One as well, though shaped for the particular needs of the community to which it came. The Christian welcome was confirmed when a number of Muhammad's followers, a few years before the Muslim community's full *hegira* from Mecca in 622, fled from Quraysh persecution to Abyssinia. The Christian *negus,* or king, of that country welcomed the refugees as co-believers and protected them.

In affirming the monotheistic orientation shared in common by Muslims and Christians, as well as by Jews, the Qur'an refers to all three communities as "People of the Message," a phrase often translated as "People of the Book." "Book" is misleading, however, since the common element the Qur'an is referring to is not an object (a particular piece of writing or collection of writings) but the prophetic message given over the ages to all human communities commanding them to love God and to serve God's creation. The divine message itself is the extension to the full human community of the question God addressed individually to the "seed of Adam": "Am I not your Cherisher and Sustainer?" Members of each human community as they form through history are given, through prophetic reminder, the chance to affirm group allegiance to their original commitment to acknowledge God alone as their Cherisher and Sustainer. Yet while this common message has been delivered to all human communities, it has been handed down in a particularly forceful and complete way by the greatest of the prophets: by Moses for the Jews, by Jesus for the Christians, and now by Muhammad for the Muslims.

It is important to keep in mind the Qur'an's view of the commonalty of the "Message" when evaluating the growing disparity of the Qur'anic attitude toward Christians. For once the Muslim community reached Medina and began to become a political entity capable of defending itself, its relations to other communities, including Christian communities, became more complicated. Some Christian communities Muslims came in contact with during this period were unwelcoming. Others were lax in worship and practice, even idolatrous (turning their wealth or ascetic perfectionism into idols).

And then we saw in chapter 2 how the Christian doctrine of the Trinity became a stumbling block to Muslims, given their rigorously monotheistic vision. In those verses where the Qur'an confronts this stumbling block, its tone toward Christians becomes pained, even aggrieved. For while Christians, in the Qur'an's view, show many signs of true devotedness to God, they tend to succumb to the dangerously extravagant temptation to turn their honored prophet Jesus into an idol by insisting that he is divine. God can no longer be One if he is "associated" (*shirk*) with a second god, a "son," born of yet a third god, Mary, in an unholy triad of gods. In the Qur'an's view, Christianity is like a revered older brother whose weaknesses undermine his worthiness as a moral guide to his younger Muslim brother. For the Qur'an is striving to pull that younger brother away from the polytheistic temptations in which he had previously been mired. Hence the Qur'an appears to be a mixture of admiration and warning when speaking of an older but errant family member.

Scriptural Support in the Qur'an for Muslim-Christian Solidarity

While the Qur'an finds much both to praise and to criticize in Christians and in Christianity, it places its greatest emphasis on the call to faith and action that all "People of the Message" share:

> To each one of your communities we have given a law and a way of life. If God had wanted to unify you all into a single community, He would have done so. But He has not done so, wanting instead to test you according to what He has given each of you. So strive together as in a race to do works of justice. To God you shall all return. At that time He will explain to you all these matters about which you now dispute. (Sura al-Ma'idah 5:48)

This extraordinary verse, and others like it, shows that religious difference isn't in essence a human invention but is instead God's will, a phenomenon instituted by God — as the Qur'an expresses it in Sura al-Hujurat 49:13 — "in order that you might come to understand each other." Religious difference, far from a curse on humankind, is actually the stimulus to mutual human enlightenment. Sameness could not educate humankind in the way God desires. Nor could sameness provoke the competition in doing the works of justice that are God's true tests of faith. Doctrinal correctness can be validated only by the quality of the deeds it inspires:

> Those who believe, Muslims, Jews, Christians, and Sabaeans — whoever believe in God and the Last Day and do works of justice — they shall receive their reward from their Cherisher and Sustainer. They shall have nothing to fear, nor shall they grieve. (Sura al-Baqarah 2:62)

A corollary of such verses is that all religious communities, including the Muslim community, are measured by the same behavioral standard. No religious community, not even that of Muhammad, "owns" God's favor simply by declaring that its beliefs are correct. "The Qur'an's reply to exclusivist claims and claims of proprietorship over God's guidance," says Muslim scholar Fazlur Rahman, "is unequivocal: Guidance is not the function of the communities but of God and good people, and *no* community may lay claims to be uniquely guided and elected. The whole tenor of the Qur'anic argument is against election."[4]

In this way the Qur'an lays the most solid ground possible for works of solidarity between and among all human communities, not just between Muslims and Christians. Yet given the Qur'an's tendency to favor the Christian community above other "People of the Message," there is reason to believe that Muslims and Christians "striving together as in a race to do works of justice" would be especially pleasing to God.

Scriptural Support for Solidarity in the New Testament

Obviously there is no direct support in the New Testament for Muslim-Christian solidarity, for the reason already mentioned. So the question is, as we have said, What can we infer about Muslim-Christian solidarity from the way the New Testament talks about other faiths?

This question is harder to ask of the New Testament than it is of the Qur'an. The Qur'an, as we just saw, sees other faiths (and especially the "People of the Message") as potentially authentic bearers of the age-old prophetic message. Yet to one degree or another all these faiths have corrupted that message by their tendency to backslide into idolatry. The Arabs, through the Prophet Muhammad, have received the ancient teaching in a clarified and final way. But they too can backslide if they are not careful. Sura at-Tauba 9:38, and other similar verses, warns Muslims that "if you turn your backs on this teaching, God will substitute another people for you who are not like you." Only by "running as in a race to do works of justice" can the various faith communities keep their eyes firmly fixed on the goal. In this sense, interfaith solidarity becomes a guarantee of fidelity to God's will.

For the New Testament, however, faith isn't a reminder of a past commitment to be perfected in the present so as to be rewarded in the future. Faith is a call to a wholly new future opened up to humankind uniquely through the death and resurrection of Jesus Christ. The New Testament's view invites all faith communities to become members of this totally new work God has revealed in and through his Son. The New Testament also in places condemns those groups, especially the Jews among whom the new religion arose, who resist or try to thwart this transformation. The Gospel of John is the clearest example of antagonism between members of the "old" and "new" testaments, dramatizing as it does the pain of the new community's expulsion from Jewish synagogues toward the end of the first century.

Yet elsewhere in the New Testament this wounded, hostile attitude toward Jews is quite different. The apostle Paul's Letter to the Romans seeks to understand God's mysterious desire to maintain the Jews in separation from the new Christian faith, the faith of converts from Judaism such as Paul himself. The forbearance toward Jews Paul preaches raises the possibility of a parallel forbearance toward other sincere monotheists — such as those called Muslims in the future — whose difference from Christians ought not to be a stumbling block. That difference might rather be seen, as Paul puts it when speaking of the continuing fidelity of Jews to their original monotheistic covenant, a sign of the "depth of the riches and wisdom of God" (Romans 11:33).

The Letter to the Romans, and in fact Paul's entire apostolic career, is also focused on broadening Christianity's appeal to a community apparently ignored by Jesus during his ministry on earth: the Gentiles of the Roman Empire. This appeal to Gentiles is actually similar to the Qur'an's appeal to the polytheists of the Arabian desert. Both Christianity and Islam invite such nonbelievers and idolaters into worship of the One God. In doing so they demand a price: the conversion of one's heart, soul, and mind, and the consequent reorientation of one's values and practices.

Yet both Christianity and Islam see conversion not as a total break from a pagan past but as a transformation of it. One of the Five Pillars of Islam itself, the *hajj,* or pilgrimage to Mecca, is the transformation of a yearly pagan rite practiced by the desert tribes. A parallel example for Christianity might be the abandonment of strict Jewish dietary laws as a symbol of the young community's embrace of the Gentile world. The apostle Peter proclaims this new orientation after having a dream in which a variety of hitherto forbidden foods is lowered from heaven. Peter concludes: "I truly understand that God shows no partiality, but in every nation anyone who fears him and does what is right is acceptable to him" (Acts 10:34–35).

Peter's breadth of vision suggests that openness to cultural and religious difference, far from weakening one's faith, actually invigorates it. Or as Paul says, "There is no distinction between Jew and Greek; the same Lord is the Lord of all and is generous to all who call on him. For everyone who calls on the name of the Lord shall be saved" (Romans 10:12). Paul's words are understood, of course, as a pledge of God's embrace of all humankind and not at all as the new religion's desire to dissolve existing human differences in the name of a vague unity. But the Qur'an no more extends such a bland invitation than Paul does. Deeds rather than dogma are the key. "Those who say, 'I love God,' and hate their brothers and sisters, are liars; for those who do not love a brother or sister whom they have seen, cannot love God whom they have not seen" (1 John 5:20).

Muslim-Christian Relations after the Qur'anic Period

Muslim-Christian relations changed rapidly as the Muslim community grew in power, particularly in its power over territories formerly controlled by Christians.

The small, embattled community that escaped to Medina in 622 was soon able to return to Mecca in triumph, taking full control of the city without bloodshed by 630. Then, within the first two decades after the Prophet's death in 632, Muslim armies swept north to capture vast sections of the Byzantine Empire. Those sections included the historic Christian cities of Damascus and Jerusalem. Muslim armies then swept out east and west. During their westward progress they captured another historic Christian center, Alexandria, on their way to the Iberian Peninsula. But in 732, one hundred years after the Prophet's death, Muslim armies were finally turned back from their advance into Europe by the forces of Charles Martel at Poitiers, in France. This confrontation set the stage for similar confrontations in the future between Muslims and those Christians living outside Muslim realms. The shadow of Poitiers hangs over the Crusades.

But for the many Christians living inside Muslim realms, whether in the Iberian Peninsula, in Egypt, in former Byzantine territories, or in Baghdad, relations with the dominant Muslim community could simply not be confrontational. Some accommodation with the new rulers had to be made. But accommodation did not entail conversion. Contrary to opinion still prevalent today, there was no "conversion by the sword." Forced conversion to Islam was prohibited ("Let there be no compulsion in religion . . ." Sura al-Baqarah 2:256). Voluntary conversion in this early period was actually discouraged, since a large influx of converts would have made both governance and defense difficult. Muslim leaders felt it safer to have Christians as well as Jews follow the Qur'anic suggestion that they "pay the poll tax (*al-jizyah*) out of hand and assume a low social profile" (Sura at-Tauba 9:29). In return they would receive the protection (*adh-dhimmah*) of the Islamic community. Consequently they would be designated "People of Protection" (*ahi adh-dhimmah*), or *dhimmi* people.

How fairly was the poll tax imposed? How oppressive was it for the "People of Protection" — the same who are called "People of the Message" in the Qur'an — to live in Muslim lands while submitting to a "low social profile"? The answer depends on time and place and circumstances. Even in cases where the *dhimmi* people's status was abused, however, these communities never experienced anything like the pogroms and persecutions suffered by Jews, Christian heretics, and pagans during Christian rule in the West. There was also some fairness in having the *dhimmi* people pay a tax for their defense. Muslims were obligated to supply that defense. They were obligated as well to pay a yearly tax of their own, *zakat,* one of the Pillars of Islam, as a way to redistribute wealth among the social classes. At its best, the *jizyah* functioned as a reasonably equitable contribution to the common good on the part of communities who found themselves in the minority.

The Growing Bonds
between Muslims and Christians

The attitudes of Christians in Muslim lands toward the invaders' religion changed over time. During the first century of Muslim rule, Christians were able to keep their distance from it. Christian pastors and theologians treated Islam simply as an Arab religion, the religion of the military conquerors, and a heretical offshoot of Christianity itself. This is how John of Damascus (c. 673–c. 749) spoke of Islam. In John's view, the Qur'an's honoring of Jesus as a human being, not as God, connected it with Arianism, the Christian heresy attacked and overthrown at the First Ecumenical Council at Nicaea in 325. While this view of Islam was harsh, it was nevertheless well-informed. John spoke Arabic and knew the Qur'an well. And it was mild compared with the view that took shape in the West, as we'll see in chapter 6.

Christians were not for long able to hold the new religion at arm's length, however. After a century of life under Muslim rule, Christians and other *dhimmi* people found themselves increasingly inclined to convert to the new religion. This change occurred not because of direct Muslim pressure but because of the greater consolidation and sophistication of the societies in which the Christians lived. Advancement in social and professional status came much more quickly if one converted to the majority religion. Islam itself was seen less and less as a Christian heresy and more and more as a distinct religion in its own right. The apologetic challenge to Christian pastors and theologians in Muslim lands became accordingly greater. They had to become much more persuasively nuanced in their arguments in favor of Christianity and in their characterizations of Islam's differences. "Unlike Christians outside of the world of Islam," says Sydney Griffiths,

> these writers, having themselves become inculturated into the life of the burgeoning Commonwealth of Islam, spoke of Islam, Muhammad, and the Qur'an from a position of thorough familiarity. They spoke knowledgeably and respectfully. While they could not accept Muhammad as a prophet, they praised him as one who "walked on the way of the prophets," and as one to be praised for having brought the polytheistic Arabs to a knowledge of the one God. They could not accept the Qur'an as scripture, but they could and did quote from it to support their own Christian beliefs. They argued that Islam was not the true religion, but they alleged that the prophetology of the Qur'an could be used to bolster the claims of Christianity to be the true religion.[5]

While inculturation meant that Christians in Muslim lands could speak far more knowledgably of Islam than could their counterparts in the West, it also meant that they increasingly spoke of their own religion in the language now dominant in their regions, in Arabic, in the language of the Qur'an itself. This shift from Greek to Arabic meant that Christianity's differences from Islam had to be expressed in a vocabulary not only shared but shaped by the majority religion. Griffiths points out a negative aspect of Christians' linguistic inculturation:

> [Inculturation brought about] a measure of cultural estrangement between the Christians of the Islamic world and the Greek and Latin speaking Christians living outside of that

world. . . . It erected a barrier of cultural, and even of theological mutual misapprehension between the Christians of the Islamic east and those living in the west.[6]

But on the positive side, Christian linguistic inculturation allowed for Christians' integration within the Muslim world and for their capacity to address their differences with the dominant religion in much more refined ways than in the starkly black-and-white confrontational style of Western apologists. We need to know more than we do about the accomplishments of such Christian apologists of this period. Such knowledge might help us resolve our continuing tendency in the West to adopt us-versus-them attitudes toward Muslims and their religion.

Christian-Muslim Cross-Fertilizations: The Abbasid Period

One great accomplishment of Christian thinkers in the Muslim world has long been clear, however. During the flowering of the Abbasid Caliphate in Baghdad from the eighth through the tenth centuries, Christian pastors and theologians became major players in the preservation of Greek learning. The Abbasid Caliphate was very open to that learning. This is no surprise given the high value the Qur'an places on reason, a value still unappreciated not only by many in the West but also by some Muslims themselves. (Pope Benedict XVI's Regensburg speech — to be discussed in chapter 7 — is a sad instance of this lack of appreciation.)

With their knowledge of Greek, Christian thinkers were able to satisfy the curiosity of enlightened Abbasid caliphs like Harun al-Rashid (763–809) by using their newly acquired Arabic to translate the works of classical philosophers, mathematicians, and physical scientists. Among these were Galen, Plotinus, and especially Aristotle. Some of the Christians, like Hunayn ibn Ishaq (809–73) and Yahya ibn 'Adi (893–974), are still known for the high quality of their Arabic translations and commentaries. They were inspired by and inspired in their turn Muslim philosophers whose names are even better known in the West than theirs, notably al-Kindi (801–73), al-Farabi (870–950), Ibn Sina (Avicenna, 980–1037), and Ibn Rushd (Averroes, 1126–98). Thanks to the talents and efforts of these great Muslims (two of whom, Avicenna and Averroes, Dante honors by placing in Limbo along with Plato and Aristotle), Greek learning was preserved, creatively reinterpreted, and eventually reintroduced to the West in the thirteenth century.

Christian-Muslim Cross-Fertilizations: The Córdoba Period

The greatest crossroad of East-West, Muslim-Christian intellectual exchange was not located in Baghdad, however, but in Córdoba, Spain, the seat of the Umayyad Caliphate of Al-Andalus from 756 to 1031. Christians and Jews served in key positions in the Caliphate and all spoke Arabic, the new regime's lingua franca. The use of Arabic, a vernacular tongue, instead of Latin, a language of the past, was in itself an immense achievement. One result was that the Greek classical heritage translated into Arabic in Baghdad quickly became available to Christians and Jews living in the Iberian Peninsula. New agricultural and economic models invented at Córdoba spread abroad quickly thanks to the prevalence of the new vernacular. Poetry experienced a renaissance as well. Composing their lyrics in Arabic encouraged poets to throw off the shackles of outmoded Latin forms and eventually to embrace and develop poetry in other vernacular idioms.

The *Divine Comedy,* by Dante Alighieri (1265–1321), is the greatest example of such influence. Composed not in Latin but in Italian, a vernacular competing with Arabic, the *Comedy* can also be seen, as scholar Muriel Mirak Weissbach attests, as "Dante's dialogue-response to Islam."[7] Seeking by means of his poem to establish the worldview for a Christian nation-state, Dante transforms key elements of Muslim faith into Christian terms. Chief among these is his reimagining of Muhammad's *mir'aj,* or ascent to heaven, sketched briefly in the Qur'an but elaborated in hadith and Muslim legend, into Dante the Pilgrim's rise through the celestial spheres to encounter the Holy Trinity itself.

Even after the Córdoba Caliphate fell and Muslim rule fragmented into independent city-states, or *taifas,* Andalusian culture continued to flourish. After Córdoba, Muslim city-states like Toledo became centers of classical and modern learning. Latin translations of Arabic versions of Aristotle as well as the works of all the great Arabic-speaking scholars, Muslim, Christian, and Jewish, made their way into Europe from Toledo, stimulating the rebirth of learning at the University of Paris in the twelfth and thirteen centuries.

Even when those Muslim states were taken over by Christian rulers, as was Toledo by Alphonso the Wise (1221–84), they continued to embrace and disseminate the best of Andalusian culture. So persistent was the culture's creativity that when Muslim rule shrank to the dimensions of a single city, Granada, in the fifteenth century, Andalusian architectural artistry and technical sophistication flowered in Granada's Alhambra. Not even when the Christian monarchs Ferdinand and Isabella took possession of Granada in 1492, and then later, in 1501, expelled all Muslims not only from Granada but from Spain itself, did Andalusian culture reach an end. The Christian monarchs entered their captured city wearing Muslim robes and preserved the Alhambra as their personal retreat. And there it remains today, a still vital remnant of what the Christian nun Hroswitha had said centuries before of Córdoba, that it was the "ornament of the world."[8]

What Baghdad and Córdoba
Can Tell Muslims and Christians Today

Social conditions were such both in Baghdad and especially in Córdoba that Muslims and Christians began to fulfill the Qur'anic commandment that they "strive together as in a race to do works of justice." The benefits of their competition are clear to see. Their differences were not erased by this competition and, in some cases, they were even sharpened. But even at their sharpest, Muslim and Christian competition benefited by cultural and linguistic sharing. Dante opposed Islam, but he was very familiar with the religion and the high culture that had been stimulated by it. Religious difference worked as a stimulant, not as a stumbling block.

The story of Muslim-Christian relations in Al-Andalus is not a simple one, however. At least it is not simply positive. Inter-religious violence played its sorry role in Al-Andalus as well. For now, though, enough has been said to complicate the picture often painted in our media, that Islam and Christianity are somehow "fated" to lock together in apocalyptic conflict according to the scenario of an inevitable "clash of civilizations." The picture is no more simply positive than it is simply negative. Muslims and Christians both believe they have been granted the gift of free will by a gracious God mercifully guiding them along the right path to *salaam, shalom,* fullness of life. The goal has not yet been reached. But the lessons of Baghdad and Córdoba should show both Muslims and Christians that despair of reaching it cannot be part of God's plan.

Discussion Questions

1. Explain why the Qur'an's attitude toward Christians is "rather ambiguous."

2. Discuss why the Qur'an sees religious difference as instituted by God. What are the benefits of religious difference in Islamic thought?

3. Muslim-Christian relations changed rapidly as the early Muslim community grew in power. Compare this development with the history of the early Christian church.

4. What are the positive and negative results of Christians in Muslim lands using Arabic as the language of intellectual discourse?

5. What were the highlights of the Christian-Muslim cross-fertilization of the "Córdoba Period"?

Chapter 6

CONFRONTING OUR DEMONS:
SIN AS EXCLUSION

As already mentioned, we can't say with certainty what Francis and the Sultan said and did during Francis's week-long stay at the Sultan's tent in Damietta. Neither man wrote or authorized an account of what transpired between them. Francis's companion, Illuminato, was the only Christian witness, but he left no written record of the event. Other Christian writers claimed later to have spoken with Illuminato about what went on, but those writers' version of what Illuminato said differ. The differences reflect either the writers' own biases or Illuminato's own struggle to keep his memories straight or both. In any case, the job of sorting through rival versions of what happened at Damietta has become, especially during the last few decades, a challenging one.

The "Official" Account of Events at Damietta:
A Victory over the Sultan and Islam

The challenge has arisen because of growing skepticism about the "official" account of what went on at Damietta, which appears in St. Bonaventure's thirteenth-century biography of Francis, entitled *The Major Legend of Saint Francis*. St. Bonaventure presents a very different Francis from the one portrayed in our book. St. Bonaventure's Francis is a spiritual version of Bishop Pelagius — a Holy Warrior bent on triumphing over the faith of the Other by a material sign of domination. In the case of Francis, the weapon is personal sanctity rather than force of arms, but the hoped-for end result is the same: the Enemy's abject capitulation.

In 1266 the Franciscans' General Chapter voted to make Bonaventure's *The Major Legend of Saint Francis,* written nearly forty years after Francis's death in 1226, the authorized version of his life and to destroy all previous accounts. What motivated the Chapter's violent effort to suppress all competitors? The likely cause of the Chapter's decision was fear, fear that convinced the brothers that they had to reshape, even distort, the most probable account of the meeting of Francis and the Sultan in order to assure their Order's very survival.

Their fear was not unfounded. The Inquisition, active at this time, was viewing the Franciscan Order with increasing suspicion. Opposition to the Crusade was a sign of heresy. Some of the brothers had already been disciplined for preaching a spiritual revival in which the hierarchy would no longer be necessary. In order to protect the Order from Vatican censure or worse, Bonaventure refocused Francis's life and vision to emphasize the saint's mystical piety and his obedience to papal decree. This isn't to say that Francis did *not* exhibit such piety or that he did *not* value obedience. It is to say that by emphasizing those characteristics to the exclusion of others, Bonaventure erased the copious evidence of Francis's openness, creativity, and desire for peacemaking. And with them disappeared any suggestion that Francis might have behaved less than confrontationally with the Sultan.

Bonaventure succeeded in his mission of saving the Franciscan Order from suppression and ruin. He did not succeed, however, in ridding the world of all previous records of Francis's life. Copies of Thomas of Celano's two previous biographies of Francis survived, as did early accounts by the Crusade preacher James of Vitry and by the French Crusader who wrote *The Chronicle of Ernoul.* These and other surviving testimonies form the basis for the view of the meeting between Francis and the Sultan that we are presenting in this book. (In the next chapter we'll summarize the hints these sources give us about what really happened during Francis's and the Sultan's time together at Damietta.)

A Trial by Fire?

In his zeal to cleanse the reputation of Francis and to rescue the Order, Bonaventure inserted into *The Major Legend* a dramatic event intended to satisfy the Vatican demand that Francis be seen as a spiritual Crusader. *The Major Legend* describes Francis as proposing to the Sultan a trial by fire between himself and the Sultan's religious advisors in order to determine whether Christianity or Islam was the true faith.

Bonaventure's insertion fired Christian imaginations already inflamed by decades of crusading. Visual artists couldn't resist elaborating the image of Francis's proposal to a degree to which not even Bonaventure himself was willing to go. For *The Major Legend* says that the Sultan, anticipating Francis's triumph, never allowed the contest to occur. Yet Giotto di Bondonne paints the raging flames in works that appear in Assisi's Basilica of St. Francis and in Florence's Basilica of the Holy Cross. Lesser artists followed Giotto's lead in flaming versions of their own. The eye-catching picture of a triumphant Francis on one side of a blazing fire, of fearfully retreating Muslim *mullas* on the other, and of a Sultan looking on in despair was too desirable not to be true.

Yet just as there was almost certainly no such fire, so too there was almost certainly no trial by it. One reason for believing no such trial by fire occurred is that no other report besides Bonaventure's so much as mentions it. In addition, the practice of such trials had been condemned by the Fourth Lateran Council in 1215. Francis, eager to obey the church when his conscience allowed him, would not have been the one to flout the Council's explicit decree.

Thirdly, Francis would not have been able to propose such a violent confrontation with the Enemy without violating his own prescriptions for dealing with Muslims. Here are those prescriptions as they appear in his 1221 *Earlier Rule* for his Order:

> The brothers who go [to Muslim lands] can conduct themselves among them spiritually in two ways. One way is to

avoid quarrels or disputes and to be subject to every human creature for God's sake, so bearing witness to the fact that they are Christians. Another way is to proclaim the word of God openly, when they see that it is God's will, calling on their hearers to believe in God almighty, Father, Son, and Holy Spirit, the Creator of all, and in the Son, the Redeemer and Savior, that they may be baptized and become Christians.[1]

Nothing in these words supports the picture of Francis aggressively goading the Sultan's clerics into a trial by fire. Instead, Francis teaches that the best way for his brothers to bring Muslims to Christ is to preach by personal example and, if they must preach in words, to be discerning in picking the occasion.

Under pressure from Pope Honorius III, however, the passage above was expunged in the later *Rule* of 1223. The only advice given there to the brothers about dealing with Muslims was that they ask permission from their superiors before traveling to Muslim lands. So even before his death in 1226 Francis's revolutionary openness to the Enemy was being erased. Forty years later, in 1266, the date when *The Major Legend* became the authorized account of Francis's life, the erasures had been filled in with wholly new words describing a very different Francis and a very different approach to the Muslim Other.

Was Bonaventure to Blame?

From our present standpoint it is easy to blame Bonaventure for what looks like willful manipulation of Francis's story. Yet, as we've indicated, the threat hanging over the Franciscan Order's continued existence was real. If Bonaventure had not reconstructed Francis's actions and intentions as he did, the Order would almost certainly have been suppressed. What the consequences of such suppression would have been for the later development of the Christian faith is anyone's guess, but it is hard to feel good about them. We might have known very little about Francis and his Franciscans today, except as obscure victims of the Inquisition. A world without Francis would be a shrunken world indeed, and not just for those of us concerned to foster Muslim-Christian relations. But our own loss would be great. We would not be able to refer to Francis, as we do in this book, as an inspiring example to Christians, as well as to Muslims, of what it means to live as a peacemaker. If Bonaventure's *The Major Legend* has kept Francis alive in the world's imagination, the end may in this case justify the means.

But what of the church? Isn't the church the real villain of the piece? Isn't the church to blame, not only for the crime of threatening to suppress this apostle of peacemaking, but also for the much greater crime of inciting the Crusades themselves — of cultivating a climate of violence to which Francis's peacemaking became the authentically Christian antidote?

Acknowledging Our Brokenness

Christians, including Catholic Christians, should not be afraid to tackle uncomfortable questions like these. Nor should they be afraid to tackle them together with today's Muslims, whose ancestors were the Enemies of the Crusaders. The questions cannot be avoided by adherents of any institutionalized religion. But tackling these hard questions means being able to do what Francis did: We have not only to tolerate but even to embrace the brokenness and moral ambiguity inherent in human affairs. For example, while we can easily point to the church's sins in fomenting the Crusades, and to its specific sin in suppressing the efforts of Francis to embody a very different response to the Muslim Enemy, we have to acknowledge that this same Francis loved the church, sinful as it was, and spent his life in service to it. His love was not a blind devotion to an ideological idol, however, but a response born of gratitude to that same church for preserving the memory of Christ's mandate to love the Enemy and for sacramentally enabling its members to embody that memory in their own lives and conduct. So, although by acting as a peacemaker at

Damietta Francis might have seemed to be defying church authority, he was also and just as faithfully following that authority by
loving the Enemy.

But another and perhaps more difficult part of what it meant
for Francis to be a peacemaker was his willingness to bear in his
own person the burden of the church's contradictory teachings.
The trials he faced to preserve the ideals of his new order from
Vatican pressure in the years after Damietta must in some ways
have been worse than those he faced in his interview with Bishop
Pelagius prior to crossing the battlefields at Damietta on his way
to the Sultan's tent. Yet he never seems to have reacted impa-
tiently and resentfully as people often do when caught in conflicts
of allegiance. He did not lash out at the church in condemna-
tion, in that way imitating the church's own violence. Instead,
he accepted the incoherence of the church's teaching as evidence
of the sinfulness that only Christ's love could heal. That he did
so is testimony to how well he had absorbed the lesson learned
by loving the Enemy — that we live in a mixed world, where no
one, not even a Francis of Assisi, can claim a moral high ground
and use it to accuse the rest of humankind of faults the accuser
himself does not embody to some degree.

Eliminating the Notion of the "Enemy"

We can see now that the incoherence of the church's teaching at
this time had much to do with its conflicted attitude toward the
Enemy. The "Enemy" had to be eliminated — the church was clear
about that. But how to do it? Various ways opened up, ways sit-
uated between two extremes. At one extreme, the Enemy was to
be eliminated by force; at the other extreme, by love. The crusading impulse embodied the first extreme. Claiming goodness and
holiness for itself, the church here named as Enemy not only Muslims, but also pagans, Jews, and heretics, all of whom were outside
the pale of humanity because they were by definition Enemies of
Christ. Exterminating them seemed justified by the language of
holy warfare, even though such language is used for quite a different purpose in some parts of the New Testament, especially in

the letters of the apostle Paul. Oneness in Christ was won by the eradication of all those who stubbornly opposed that unity.

At the other extreme, the Enemy was to be eliminated by love. Eliminating the Enemy by loving him is not to exterminate the person or group, however. It is to eliminate the notion of Enemy itself. Evil does not disappear. The difference is that it no longer resides exclusively in the Other. Evil comes into view now as an affliction borne to one degree or another by all humanity, not just by isolated groups or individuals. This is because by loving the Enemy Christians see more clearly that all are one in Christ. Unity in this case is measured not by the usual human categories of religious belief or political interest or ethnic identity, but by common membership in God's human creation — or, as Christians express it, in the Body of Christ (where that Body is understood to include all humanity, not just church-approved parts of it.).

Despite appearances, there is no moral equivalence between these opposed ways of eliminating the Enemy. Elimination by love and elimination by violence are not two sides of one coin or two extreme alternatives within a field of plausible choices. They indicate the boundaries of what God wills and doesn't will for us. Or more accurately put: They indicate the boundary of true being on the one hand and of negation of being on the other. Elimination of the Enemy by violence is a fundamentally self-destructive act whose end is ugliness, futility, and nothingness. Elimination of the Enemy by violence magnifies within us the evil we attempt to exclude. Elimination of the Enemy by love is fundamentally beautiful, purposeful, and creative; it transforms the evil within and outside us into evil's opposite.

Acknowledging the Enemy Within

Muslims and Christians engaging in projects for the common good have to accept the evil for which they're both responsible, and they have to do this together, as a shared discipline. They have to share as well their struggles with the temptation to take the easy way out, seeking apparent safety from each other by assuming for themselves a stance of moral purity. Given the continuing violence of their common history, this sharing will not be easy. Something in them will always be whispering in their ear: "You alone have the truth. Those other people are liars, or at least they're deluded. Look at their insulting beliefs about God! Look at the crimes they've committed in His name!" It's hard to admit that sometimes we have the truth, but that at other times we don't; or that we both do and don't have it at the same time. The questions Christ asks in Matthew 7:3–5 are ones Christians and Muslims can profitably (if not comfortably) ask of themselves and of each other: "Why do you see the speck in your neighbor's eye, but do not notice the log in your own? Or how can you say to your neighbor, 'Let me take the speck out of your eye,' while the log is in your own eye?" Christians and Muslims can then weigh the wisdom of Christ's own answer to those questions: "You hypocrite, first take the log out of your own eye, and then you will see clearly to take the speck out of your neighbor's."

But Christians and Muslims have to accept and embrace the good they have done and continue to do as well. The evidence for this good won't dazzle the eye the way evil will. A ball of flame separating Francis from the Sultan makes for a catchier painting than the mutual admiration that bound the men like brothers. But the admiration is real; the ball of flame an illusion. For always when we resist the temptation to demonize the Other and to embrace him or her instead we are entering the realm of the real. The Qur'an puts this truth in the form of an injunction:

> For beauty and goodness and fullness are not at all the equal opposites of ugliness and evil and emptiness; so repel evil with goodness, and then the person between whom and you there is hatred will become your warmest supporter and friend. (Sura Fussilat 41:34)

"Between whom and you there is hatred. . . ." The Qur'an's phrasing is exactly right. The wall we erect to keep ourselves safe within the realm of self-assumed moral purity and the Other locked up in the un-realm of evil is the product of our uncontrolled passions, primarily of our fears. The wall has no other basis to stand on than those uncontrolled passions. The passions themselves are morally neutral. Whether they become destructive, or whether they serve what is good and beautiful in us, depends on how we direct them. But it is because we have such imperfect control over them that we live in a broken world of our own making. Sometimes we can summon our strength to love the Enemy, sometimes we can't. There is no Muslim or Christian, and certainly no Muslim or Christian community, that is not caught up in this struggle.

Once they've achieved a high level of trust with each other, Muslims and Christians can learn to report candidly and undefensively to each other their own and their forebears' struggles to "repel evil with goodness." Sometimes those struggles will have ended successfully, but perhaps more often they will not. Both groups have at various times over the centuries fallen into the trap of demonizing the Other. Bonaventure's determination to manipulate Francis's meeting with the Sultan into a victory celebration is unfortunately typical of the way Christians as well as Muslims have portrayed their encounters over the centuries. Neither religion can claim to have often taken the high road of reconciliation in their dealings with each other. What's more, the past's sorry record continues today. Mutual demonization has not gone out of style.

Religion, a Cause of Violence?

We'll look soon at some contemporary examples of such demonization. But there's a question people often ask that requires explicit treatment first. Doesn't demonization of the Other actually have its *source* in Christianity and in Islam, as many commentators have recently claimed? We can talk all we want about the fact that following the prophetic commandment to love God and neighbor leads us to *salaam*, fullness of life, while ignoring or spurning it leads us to futility and emptiness. But in fact Christians and Muslims have in the past and in the present behaved as if doing just the opposite — ignoring the commandment — were actually the center of their faith. How do we, the authors of this book, square our claims for Christianity's and Islam's rejection of violence (except in well-defined situations of self-defense) with the historical record of flesh-and-blood Christians and Muslims who embraced it?

Being clear on this point is important. If Christianity and Islam are sources of violence, then we are all in for a lot of trouble. But if the source lies outside the two religions and if in fact the religions are God's gifts to enable Muslims and Christians to overcome that violence, then they have every reason to work hard together for the common good. Their religions would compel them to do so.

Sin as Exclusion

Answering the question about the source of violence means talking about sin. Christianity and Islam view the weight and effect of human sin very differently. Christianity teaches that the sin of Adam and Eve not only brought ruin to themselves and to their entire progeny, but that it had a calamitous effect as well on all creation. In Islam, sin is a grave danger for each individual, but it is not inherited (or "original," meaning "from the origin"). Nor are the effects of sin cosmic in scope. Great and perhaps as unbridgeable as these differences are, however, we can still say that Islam and Christianity view sin itself similarly: as exclusion — as humanity's willful building of a wall of hatred between itself and God and between itself and the Other. As such, sin is nothing but negativity. It is the willful rejection of the fundamental commandment, handed down by all the prophets, to worship God and serve God's creation. Christianity and Islam, and Judaism as well, call humanity back from its slide into defiance and division toward self-yielding and wholeness.

In both Christianity and Islam this slide is encouraged by the spirit of division, Satan himself (*Shaitan,* in Arabic). It is true that Satan is given different degrees of power in the two religions. In Christianity Satan is given the power to tempt even God as evidenced in his temptation of Jesus in the desert. In Islam Satan's power affects human beings alone. But in both scriptures Satan's desire is to dominate his victim by encouraging a spirit of domination like his own. In Matthew 4:8 and in Luke 4:5–7, Satan promises Jesus "all the kingdoms of the world . . . if you will fall down and worship me." In Sura an-Nas 114:5, Shaitan "whispers into the hearts of humankind" a constant stream of schemes for getting the better of others. The human capacity for contempt that Shaitan arouses mirrors Shaitan's own contempt for humankind itself. Shaitan (who in Islam is not an angel created of spirit but a *djinn,* an intelligent being created of a lesser material, fire) refuses to obey God's command that *djinns* and angels both must acknowledge human authority. "I am not the sort to bow down to a human being, a thing you created from clay, molding them from mud," Satan asserts to God (Sura al-Hijr 15:34), in a gesture that has rightly been called racist.

The stories about Satan that belong to both Christianity and Islam remind us that in both scriptures our need to resist the sin of exclusion is urged not through philosophical argument, but through dramas of personal encounter between Creator and creation. It is these accounts of God's direct intervention in human history at particular times and places and in particular people and communities that reveal sin through concrete events rather than through moral abstractions.

We see vividly in both scriptures how sin produces a blindness in individuals that prevents them from acknowledging their indebtedness to God and their kinship with others. Ego and power-over dominate and blight the lives of individuals. Examples abound. Muslims will instantly recall the Qur'an's portrait of Pharaoh; Christians will instantly recall the New Testament's portrait of Herod.

We also see vividly portrayed in both scriptures the social consequences of the sinful behavior of individuals, a linkage particularly noticeable in the case of national leaders like the two just named, Pharaoh and Herod. We see the emergence of unjust, exclusionary structures that entrap many in lives of misery and poverty at the expense of the powerful few. The Qur'an's

Meccan suras refer to Pharaoh's sinfulness in order to highlight the similarly unjust practices of the Quraysh: their enrichment of themselves through Mecca's pilgrimage and caravan trade and their indifference to those less privileged than themselves. The Qur'an also evokes the enmity the Prophet Muhammad suffered in bringing this critique to his tribesmen. Likewise, the Gospels speak loud and clear of how Jesus identified with the marginalized and of the enmity such solidarity caused him on the part of the powerful.

Jesus and the Prophet Muhammad: Alike in Suffering Sin as Exclusion

Without in any way wanting to confuse Jesus with the Prophet Muhammad in terms of their identities (whether divine and human or human only), we can still say that both suffered in their earthly lives from sin as exclusion.

The New Testament understands the scapegoating and suffering of Jesus on the cross as the ultimate sign of his solidarity with the poor in their exclusion by the rich. Not only is Jesus physically destroyed; he is spat upon and ridiculed, just as the poor are. In every dimension of his human nature he experienced, as the poor do in every dimension of theirs, the full effects of the elimination of the Other through violence. Yet Christians also see in this sign of solidarity, terrible as it is, an even more powerful sign of hope. For the crucified one, in Christianity's view, is not merely a man, and not merely even a heroic man. As human, Jesus becomes one with us in our sin and suffering; as God, he transforms our sin and suffering into glorious life in which all share who open themselves to this grace.

The Qur'an will not, of course, go so far. It insists that God would never allow one of His beloved prophets to experience the shame of crucifixion. But it equally insists that Jesus was indeed scapegoated and brought to the cross. God then intervened to save him bodily from a shameful death. How exactly that rescue was accomplished is a question the Qur'an is not interested in explaining, for the Qur'an's interest is in pinpointing the social and spiritual dynamic that led to Jesus' mistreatment:

> Here are the reasons why the People of the Message, or the Jews, have incurred God's anger: Because they broke their Covenant, and because they did not believe God's signs and warnings, and because they killed the prophets against all justice, and because they boasted, "Our hearts have sealed up all truth inside them." — No, not at all! It is God who has sealed up their hearts for their defiant self-sufficiency. Only a very few of them are open to God. And more reasons still: because they rejected faith, and because they slandered Mary, the mother of 'Isa, claiming that she was a fornicator. And because they said in their pride, "Look! We have killed 'Isa, son of Mary and Messenger of God!" (Sura Nisa' 4:155–57)

Please note that the Qur'an's indictment of the Jews is not generic. The Jews "have incurred God's anger" not because they are Jews but because many of them — but not all — have rejected God's offer of covenant by closing their hearts both to God and to the Other. As a result, such Jews have become isolated within their own self-regarding tribal ethos. The bitter evidence of such self-exclusion is their killing of their own (Jewish) prophets, an action the Qur'an describes as "against all justice." The Arabic word translated here as "justice" (*haqq*) also conveys the idea of truth, and therefore also of the reality to which truth corresponds. Not only has this group broken all bonds of right human relationships. By doing so it has fallen into the darkness of un-reality, since it is no longer connected with the reality of God and God's creation. The prophets were trying to call the group back to that reality. They were scapegoated for their pains.

The Prophet Muhammad himself suffered scapegoating by being marginalized as a prophet by his own people, just as the Jewish prophets and Jesus were by theirs. But marginalization threatened him from his birth. While the Prophet Muhammad was indeed born into the ruling Quraysh tribe, his own clan, the Hashem, was obscure and relatively powerless. The death of the Prophet Muhammad's father before the Prophet was born exposed him to immediate risk, since no overarching moral law bound the tribes to care for those left without family protection. The Prophet Muhammad's life was further endangered on his mother's death during his early childhood. Fortunately he found shelter with his grandfather. But when, in later childhood, his grandfather died, the Prophet Muhammad's life was again in peril until his uncle took him in. The Prophet Muhammad never forgot these early experiences of deprivation and threat. The *hadith* (authenticated accounts of the Prophet Muhammad's words and action) tell many stories of his efforts to secure conditions of social justice both during his stay in Medina and then in Mecca itself, after his nonviolent return to and assumption of leadership in that city in 630.

God's choice of the Prophet Muhammad as his vessel of communication suggests the divine desire to establish consistency between the message and the messenger. In every way the Qur'an supports the well-being of the marginalized as against the privileges of the powerful. It speaks emphatically again and again about the community's obligation to care for orphans, widows, the homeless, and all others who have slipped from clan protection, like the Prophet Muhammad himself. Yet the fact that the Qur'an champions the dispossessed is not based on ethical reasoning alone, nor even on the Prophet's own personal experience or viewpoint. The Qur'an's championing of the poor is based on a far deeper and more powerful mandate, on God's will that we recognize our human solidarity. Nevertheless, the example of the Prophet Muhammad's concern for orphans and other social outcasts, as shown in many *hadith,* is a major grounding for Muslims' consciousness and practice of social justice.

The Sin of Exclusion and Divine Mercy

In addition to their both seeing sin as exclusion, the Qur'an and the New Testament also agree that sin leaves humankind in a perilous, ambiguous state. While prone to exclude others, we are also called to embrace them in solidarity. The nature of free will is that we are perpetually subjected to temptation even while we are surrounded by the grace needed to overcome that temptation. The divine mercy provides that grace. Our responsibility is to open ourselves to it. But to receive grace is not to possess it as a personal claim or as a reward setting us over others. For in that way the sin of exclusion reinstates itself through hypocrisy — a form of sinfulness that both the Qur'an and Jesus in the Gospels denounce vehemently.

Jesus tells a parable that depicts the extreme possibilities of human response to God's grace in terms that Muslims can assent to just as well as Christians:

> He also told this parable to some who trusted in themselves and regarded others with contempt. "Two men went up to the temple to pray, one a Pharisee and the other a tax collector. The Pharisee, standing by himself, was praying thus: 'God, I thank you that I am not like other people: thieves, rogues, adulterers, or even like this tax collector. I fast twice a week; I give a tenth of all my income.' But the tax collector, standing far off, would not even look up to heaven, but was beating his breast and saying, 'God, be merciful to me, a sinner!' I tell you, this man went down to his home justified rather than the other, for all who exalt themselves will be humbled, but all who humble themselves will be exalted." (Luke 18:9–14)

Mounting the high ground of moral exclusivism, the Pharisee fancies himself able to point to evil as a condition totally outside himself. In his opinion, the struggle with temptation within himself, at least, has come to a successful conclusion. But in fact he has entered into a state "against all justice" and against all reality as well. The more loudly he asserts his righteousness, the less visible he becomes as a member of God's creation. As for the tax collector, his admission of sinfulness and his cry for mercy "exalted" him within that creation. Knowing himself to be flawed, he yet calls out for wholeness. He accepts the ambiguity of his situation, hoping for its favorable resolution, but knowing that such resolution lies not in human hands but in those of God.

Modern Parallels with the Pharisee and the Tax Collector

Christians and Muslims reflecting on the words and behavior of the crusading church on the one hand and the words and behavior of both Francis and the Sultan on the other will find useful parallels in the parable just quoted. But they can also find useful parallels in the words and behavior of their contemporaries. They can point to many examples where contemporary Christians and Muslims who recognize God's love for all God's creation, not just a certain part of it, are working together for the common good, just as Francis and the Sultan did. *Horizons* magazine, published by the Islamic Society of North America (ISNA), faithfully publicizes such efforts among Muslims and Christians. In these accounts, the people involved, "standing far off" like the tax collector, call upon God's mercy to help them do the good work He has ordained for them.

Yet despite the great number and effectiveness of such interfaith groups, they attract almost no attention from the media. What attracts the media instead are examples of the opposite — of Christians and Muslims using their religion to hasten exclusion, not to overcome it. It's not that such bad examples don't exist. Alas, they do. Christians and Muslims reflecting on Luke's parable will also find many such instances where their co-religionists "stand apart from others" like the Pharisee and do all in their power to erect walls of exclusion between themselves and the feared Other. Those walls permit dehumanization, scapegoating, and, eventually, direct violence against the Other.

The question is not whether such terrible examples of supposedly religious violence exist, for they do. The question is whether it is either Islam or Christianity that truly motivates them. Or to put the question in an expanded way: Is the Islam or Christianity that seems to motivate those examples truly Islam or Christianity, as we have been describing them here? Or have the two religions been transformed into political ideologies and enlisted in the service of motives that are starkly at odds with truly religious ones?

Are Today's Crusaders Christian? Are Today's Terrorists Muslim?

Here is the place where Muslims and Christians have to acknowledge the effect that the tragic events of September 11, 2001, have had upon their views of each other. The men who hijacked the airplanes on that day and drove them into the World Trade Center and the Pentagon were raised as Muslims. Osama bin Ladin, the mastermind of this heinous act, claimed that he was doing God's will, in accordance with a completely baseless interpretation of *jihad,* which made possible the killing of innocents.

By making such claims, Bin Ladin turned Islam into an instrument of violent exclusion, a hideous distortion instantly accepted as reality by his Enemy. President Bush, the Congress, and the media reacted as if Bin Ladin and Bin Ladin alone spoke for all Muslims and as if Bin Ladin's understanding of Islam were the true one. Muslims everywhere quickly found themselves under suspicion, and Islam itself was seen as a violent religion.

A cruel irony began to emerge. By accepting Bin Ladin's distortion of Islam as the true version, the Christian political and religious leaders of the United States ended up distorting Christianity itself. In his declaration that by engaging in "preventive war" against Iraq he was doing battle with the "axis of evil," President Bush was speaking very much in crusading language. He used that language explicitly in an unscripted comment made shortly after September 11, warning Americans that "this crusade, this war on terrorism, is going to take awhile." The term "crusade" caused such a furor abroad, however, that Bush's advisors made sure he never employed it again.

But in other comments Bush continued to portray himself, as the popes had done, as God's chosen scourge of the evil Other. According to the Israeli newspaper *Haaretz* (June 26, 2003), Bush told Palestinian Prime Minister Abbas that "God told me to strike Al Qaeda and I struck them, and then he instructed me to strike at Saddam, which I did." To do President Bush credit, he affirmed later that Islam was in reality a religion of peace, but by that time the damage had been done, and continues to be done. At the time of this book's writing, nearly a decade after September 11, the United States is conducting wars in two Muslim-dominant countries, Iraq and Afghanistan, and may soon be involved in a third, in Iran.

And what do American Christians think about Islam as a result of the ongoing trauma of war? According to a 2007 Pew Research Study, 70 percent of Christians say that their religion has little or nothing in common with Islam (compared to 59 percent in 2005). They use words like "fanatic," "radical," and "terror" to describe Islam. Yet 58 percent of Christians also admit that they know "very little" of Islam. What they do know, they say, comes mainly through the media, which since September 11, 2001, have tended to portray Islam as a religion of suicide bombers. So it's no wonder that they have a negative view of it or that, as a 2009 LifeWay Research report indicates, two-thirds of Protestant pastors say, "Islam is a dangerous religion."[2]

Today's Challenge

Muslims and Christians joining together to do social justice projects have the task of overcoming prejudices like these. By undertaking this mission, they know exactly what they're up against: the temptation by their co-religionists to divide the world into black and white, the temptation to claim oneself as God's elect to the exclusion of others, the temptation of the Pharisee. But the temptation is one they will have to watch for in themselves as well. Insofar as they are only human, and not God, they will have to face this temptation again and again. The insidiousness of evil is that its temptation is never more potent than when we believe we have overcome it.

Muslims and Christians joining together to do social justice projects can nevertheless agree gently to warn each other when signs of the temptation appear among them. Their projects will benefit from mutual self-critique. Then they can feel truly free to affirm what they both believe, that nothing else in what they say or do together matters beyond their loving God and God alone and serving others in God's name.

Discussion Questions

1. How do you make sense of the diverse historical records of what happened at Damietta?

2. The Qur'an champions the cause of orphans, widows, the homeless, and all others who have slipped from the community's protection. Do the Jewish and Christian scriptures proclaim a similar focus?

3. Do both Islam and Christianity teach their followers to love their enemies?

4. There are many metaphors used to describe sin, such as blindness, missing the mark, and so forth. Why is "sin as exclusion" an apt metaphor for sin?

5. Identify the distortions of both Islam and Christianity in the wake of September 11, 2001.

Part IV

Working in Solidarity
for the Salaam of the Kingdom

Chapter 7

COMMON GROUND, COMMON ACTION

What Really Happened at Damietta?

According to Bonaventure's account of the meeting of Francis and the Sultan, the two men spent their time together attempting to wrestle the other, a spiritual rival, to the ground. Francis, in Bonaventure's view, emerged the victor. But for Bonaventure and the church, Francis's victory couldn't remain Francis's alone. It had to be Christianity's victory too, just as the loss couldn't be that of only the Sultan; it had to be that of Islam as well. The meaning of the encounter as proof of Christianity's superiority had to expand from its personal dimension to its widest religious and political dimensions. The pressure of external crises drove this need, including the one that threatened the Franciscan Order. A second crisis threatened the whole church, the crisis the church itself had caused by launching the Crusades. Bonaventure's *The Major Legend* successfully addressed this twofold need, but it did so only by altering or reinventing the facts of the encounter between Francis and the Sultan.

But what were those facts? As we've said, they're not easy to determine. The original sources we still possess (those not destroyed by the Franciscans) were not written by eyewitnesses, nor were the writers themselves unbiased. Thomas of Celano as well as James of Vitry and the author of *The Chronicle of Ernoul,* who were both on the Fifth Crusade, were Crusade supporters. But the fact that they were biased in this way makes more credible the evidence they inadvertently give of a peaceful encounter between Francis and the Sultan, an encounter marked neither by competitive rivalry nor by the eventual triumph of one over the other, but instead by mutual respect and openness.

Gestures of Confidence

We have already mentioned some of those gestures made during the first meeting of Francis and the Sultan. Francis's greeting, "May the Lord give you peace," would have been among the first and the calm, gracious demeanor of Francis would have been another. Thomas of Celano described Francis as "a man of cheerful countenance. . . . And because he was very humble, he showed his mildness to all men, adapting himself usefully to the behavior of all."[1] The Sultan, for his part, was a man famed for his hospitality. We have already spoken of his deep regard for ascetics, whether Sufis or Christian monks. The two men were nearly of the same age. They must at the least have been very curious about each other.

The Sultan must have wondered, for example, whether Francis had come as an emissary of the pope or the pope's armies. He must have hoped that Francis bore a favorable answer to the Sultan's appeal for peace. What we know he explicitly asked, however, was whether Francis wanted to convert to Islam. No, Francis boldly replied. He and Illuminato "would never want to become Muslims." They had come to him, Francis said, "as messengers on behalf of the Lord God, that he might turn his soul to God." The key phrase here is "messengers on behalf of the Lord God," rather than "of the pope" or even "of Jesus Christ." Francis's mission went beyond religious politics. It went beyond a direct assault on a religious difference (Christ's Sonship) guaranteed to doom all further conversation. If in the course of discussion Francis could lead the Sultan to Christ, he would indeed attempt to do so. Sincere, unforced conversion to Christianity was Francis's aim. But he must treat the Sultan as a child of God and find the keys to the "true faith" within the Sultan's own heart. Only then might he, Francis, turn those keys.

Remarkably, the Sultan was not offended either by Francis's refusal of conversion to Islam or by Francis's assumption that the Sultan himself needed conversion. Quite the opposite. Even James of Vitry, who calls the Sultan "that cruel beast," says in the same breath that Malik al-Kamil, under Francis's influence, "became sweetness itself. He kept [Francis] with him for a few days and with a great deal of attention listened to him preach the Faith of Christ to him and to his followers."[2]

James of Vitry probably saw the Sultan's "sweetness" as further proof of Francis's special power to tame wild animals. But a more reasonable interpretation sees the Sultan actually welcoming the challenge of Francis's words. Conversion, a value prized as much by Islam, where it is called *tawwab* (turning), as by Christianity, where it is called *metanoia* (a turning or change of mind), means in the deepest sense not simply a pledge of allegiance to a particular faith but even more a deepening of the faith already professed. Francis was indeed inviting the Sultan to a test of faith. But this test involved a searching of the heart, not immunity to flames.

Francis, as James of Vitry indicates, spent several days with the Sultan, where he was honored in every way. The Sultan permitted him to preach to his soldiers. This is not to be wondered at. Qur'an Sura al-'Ankabut 29:46 enjoins Muslims "to listen and respond to People of the Message (Jews and Christians) only in the fairest way — unless they are behaving maliciously." What Sultan Malik would not have allowed from Francis or any Christian preacher was insulting language used of the Prophet Muhammad or of the faith itself. The fact that the Sultan gave permission to Francis to preach clearly shows the Sultan knew and valued Francis as a true apostle of peace.

When it came time for Francis to depart, the Sultan may well have asked him to bear yet another offer of peace back to the Crusader camp. We don't know that for sure, however. What we do know for sure is the Sultan offered him gifts, all of which Francis turned down, except for one, a horn used to call the faithful to prayer. (We'll have more to say of this gift and Francis's acceptance of it in our final chapter.) But then Francis himself asked for something: a meal. This was a radical gesture on Francis's part, completely reversing the pattern of hostility toward Muslims set by the Crusaders. Breaking bread with the Enemy was Francis's way of symbolizing in the language of both religions the common bond Christians and Muslims shared as servants of God. Regrettably, Francis's gesture was eliminated in Bonaventure's "official" account and replaced by the image of the trial by fire. "This meal," says Paul Moses, "ought to have been the enduring image of the encounter between the saint and the sultan, painted in bright colors on cathedral walls."[3]

Emerging Values

This is the way the visit began and unfolded — in an atmosphere of hospitality, mutual appreciation, keen debate, prayerful openness, and gratitude. These values are prophetic. They stand starkly in opposition to the fear and prejudice driving the Crusades and debasing the religious imagination of those who took part in them. Beacons of light in the darkness, the values expressed in the encounter of Francis and the Sultan enable us to see the road ahead more clearly. They point a way forward for today's Christians and Muslims. They offer guidance in the midst of landscapes as war torn as that surrounding Damietta. They open up possibilities for interfaith solidarity in our own violent times that would perhaps have been invisible to us otherwise.

Today's Gestures of Confidence

Gestures of confidence like those expressed between Francis and the Sultan have been rare events in Muslim-Christian relations in recent times. Yet something resembling those gestures emerged recently when the highest authorities of the two faiths gathered together for a conference at the Vatican in 2008. On that occasion the authorities not only set a precedent for taking action for the common good; they also asked Muslims and Christians at the grassroots level, like the audience addressed in this book, to make sure the precedent bore fruit.

We can perhaps take some comfort that the precedent grew out of a blunder also made at the highest level. The blunder's emerging from such a lofty source shows that none of us is exempt from stumbling once in a while along the path of peacemaking. The question for everyone, whether pope or *mulla,* "ordinary" Christian or "ordinary" Muslim, is how we learn from our mistakes. The question cannot be asked, however, unless our confidence in each other is high. People nagged by fear and distrust cannot tolerate one false move on the other's part. If they feel they see proof of malevolence in the other's blunder, they instinctively react defensively. People who trust God will forgive each other's errors (and their own) and actually learn from them.

Pope Benedict's Regensburg Speech: Negative Moment, Positive Outcome

The blunder in question was a big one, and it was made by the pope himself. On September 13, 2006, Pope Benedict XVI delivered a lecture at the University of Regensburg in Germany entitled "Faith, Reason, and the University: Memories and Reflections." His purpose in this lecture was to argue for the compatibility between Christian faith and human reason. This would be a safe enough topic for one of Pope Benedict's vast background, both in Western philosophy and in Catholic theology. In order to introduce his theme, the pope followed a standard rhetorical strategy of providing a strong opening contrast. In this instance the contrasting example the pope chose was an allusion to a religion in which faith and human reason were presumably *not* compatible. Unfortunately, in making his choice Benedict reached beyond his area of expertise to locate that contrasting example in Islam.

What encouraged the pope to make this ill-advised move was a quotation he'd come across from a fourteenth-century Byzantine emperor named Manuel II Paleologus. In this quotation Paleologus asserts, "Show me just what Mohammed brought that was new, and there you will find things only evil and inhuman, such as his command to spread by the sword the faith he preached." It would have been easy for Benedict to refute such a patently false statement. Instead, after reproducing the emperor's quotation, the pope seemed to condone it, critiquing only its tone:

> The emperor, after having expressed himself so forcefully, goes on to explain in detail the reasons why spreading the faith through violence is something unreasonable. Violence is incompatible with the nature of God and the nature of the soul. . . . The decisive statement in this argument against violent conversion is this: not to act in accordance with reason is contrary to God's nature. The editor [of the text in which the Paleologus quotation occurs] observes: "For the emperor, as a Byzantine shaped by Greek Philosophy, this statement is self-evident. But for Muslim teaching, God is absolutely transcendent. His will is not bound up with any of our categories, even that of rationality." Here [the editor] quotes a work of the noted French Muslim R. Arnaldez, who points out that Ibn Hazn went so far as to state that God is not bound even by his own word, and that nothing would oblige him to reveal the truth to us. Were it God's will, we would even have to practice idolatry.[4]

Having established, at least to his own satisfaction, the point that a religion, like Islam, that divorces itself from human reason becomes prey to violence, Pope Benedict then turned to his real theme, the promotion of the idea that Christianity is quite different: it is a religion for which human reason is central and therefore violence is not only abhorrent but logically impossible. He did not mention Islam again in his speech.

The pope's defenders point out that the use of the Paleologus quotation, while unfortunate, was clearly not part of an attempt on the pope's part to discredit Islam. We can assume that this was the case, but the pope's miscalculation of the effect of even a casual reference of his to Islam was calamitous, and the damage had been done. Street protests broke out in many Muslim-dominant countries. Many Islamic politicians and religious leaders angrily objected to what they said was the pope's own endorsement of an insulting mischaracterization of Islam.[5]

In an attempt to cool passions, thirty-eight Muslim scholars wrote one month later, on October 13, 2006, "An Open Letter to the Pope," in which they calmly and fraternally corrected the errors of fact and nuance in the pope's Regensburg speech. They showed that, far from being at odds with reason, Islam actually upholds it. They pointed out that it was thanks to Islamic civilization, as we saw in chapter 5, that the learning of Greek scientists and philosophers was preserved during the West's own "Dark Ages."[6]

The Vatican for some reason never responded to this letter. But instead of reacting defensively to this failure, the scholars decided to take the initiative and to take it in the most positive direction possible. They decided to make the prophetic link between Islam and Christianity absolutely clear.

It wasn't enough, they felt, merely to correct faulty facts and assumptions. It was necessary to take a more active, creative step, one that would challenge not only the pope but also all other Christian leaders to acknowledge the deep ties they actually shared with Islam. These ties bound all three religions of Abraham together. These ties emerged from the common responsibility of Judaism, Christianity, and Islam to obey the greatest of the divine commandments: to love God and neighbor.

The result was the groundbreaking document referred to in the Introduction, "A Common Word between Us and You," endorsed by over a hundred of the world's most prominent Muslim thinkers and clerics, as well as by the king of Jordan. The document's title comes from a Qur'anic verse quoted within the document:

> Say: O People of the Scripture! Come to a common word between us and you: that we shall worship none but God, and that we shall ascribe no partner unto Him, and that none of us shall take others for lords beside God. And if they turn away, then say: Bear witness that we are they who have surrendered (unto Him). (*Sura al-'Imran* 3:64)

The Qur'anic message is addressed to both Christians and Jews ("People of the Scripture"), though the document itself is addressed only to Christians. To explain the basis for the "word" the two faiths have in common, the document cites three sources, two from the Qur'an, one from a hadith (an authenticated statement by the Prophet Muhammad). One Qur'anic source attests to God's unity: "Say: He is God, the One! / God, the Self-Sufficient Besought of all!" (*Sura al-Ikhlas* 112:1–2). The other attests to the necessity of loving Him: "So invoke the Name of thy Lord and devote thyself to Him with a complete devotion" (*Sura al-Muzzammil* 73:8). The hadith asserts the obligation to love the neighbor: "None of you has faith until you love for your neighbor what you love for yourself."

"A Common Word" cites one of the three parallels from the New Testament Gospels:

> Jesus Christ said: "'Hear, O Israel, the Lord our God, the Lord is One. And you shall love the Lord your God with all your heart, with all your soul, with all your mind, and with all your strength.' This is the first commandment. And the second, like it, is this: 'You shall love your neighbor as yourself.' There is no other commandment greater than these." (Mark 12:29–31)

The document sums up the meaning of its scriptural juxtapositions in these terms:

> Thus in obedience to the Holy Qur'an, we as Muslims invite Christians to come together with us on the basis of what is common to us, which is also what is most essential to our faith and practice: the Two Commandments of love.

Previous to the publication of "A Common Word," both Christians and Muslims would likely have understood the commandment to love God and neighbor as one given to Jews and to themselves but not to each other. But after the publication of "A Common Word," Christians and Muslims for the first time had to admit that the commandment is directed to each other as well. And they also had to admit that the commandment demands a response far more challenging than dutiful assent by Christianity's and Islam's respective religious elites. "A Common Word" shows that the divine commandment calls all worshipers of both faiths to action. The obligation to love God and neighbor is not to be diminished to the size of a topic "for polite ecumenical dialogue between selected religious leaders," as the Muslim scholars put it in the part of "A Common Word" quoted in the Introduction. While the scholars do not say specifically what else may be involved, they clearly assume that the prophetic teaching has not been honored if it does not issue in concrete deeds. Echoing *Sura al-Ma'idah* 5:48, the scholars end "A Common Word" by enjoining its readers to "vie with each other only in righteousness and good works."

The scholars also point out that this common ground of love of God and service to others is the only one suitable for building a foundation of peace between nations. Loving God and loving neighbor is placed on the world stage as the cornerstone of world peace and of the very future of the world. Religious faith, whether Christian or Muslim, is not and never has been just a question of personal salvation, of our individually "being right with God." *Solidarity* as Muslims and Christians in loving God and loving our neighbor is essential to the very future of the world and to "meaningful peace."

From Blunder to Blessing

A visit to the "A Common Word" website confirms the fact that the document has received a warm response from a great many Christian denominations. The Catholic Church, to which "A Common Word" is particularly addressed, held a special thirty-day conference at the Vatican in the fall of 2008, at which those gathered pledged to pursue together the goal of peacemaking that they are called to by the commandment to love God and neighbor. As we mentioned in our Introduction, the pope, echoing the language of the "Common Word" document, made clear in his welcoming speech that the goal could not be achieved at high level conferences alone, but that to bear fruit it must be rooted at all levels of society. We mentioned also in the Introduction the pope's urging Christians and Muslims to find common ground in praxis (a term we will define later in this chapter) rather than in theology. Peacemaking requires prayerful bonding between Muslim and Christian participants; but the focus of the bonding should be effective deeds of justice, not an unachievable theological unanimity.

The pope's Vatican speech and his subsequent words about interfaith praxis have done much to rectify the damage of Regensburg. Above all, they have done much to prevent ordinary Muslims and Christians from becoming discouraged by the apparent smallness of their own local efforts to work together. Serving the needs of our immediate neighbors may not seem as if it could have an impact on world peace, but every effort that builds bridges between people has a ripple effect in the world, like the proverbial stone dropping in the pond. Muslims and Christians are also well served by the pope's advice to aim for unity in deeds rather than in theology. Theological discussion is important, but not at the cost of forgetting to obey God's word, or of making religious solidarity contingent upon prefect theological harmony.

A pope's blunder has become a blessing. It's time for Muslims and Christians everywhere, young or old, rich or poor, socially advantaged or the opposite, to transform that blessing into concrete actions that bring peace to a broken world.

Moving toward Praxis: The Centrality of Social Justice

We spoke in chapters 3 and 4 about the centrality of social justice in both Christianity and Islam. Here, as Christians and Muslims move toward embodying this principle in concrete actions, we'll synthesize these teachings so that Muslims and Christians will be able to speak confidently in one voice about why joint action for the common good is enjoined upon them.

Unanimity in this respect is essential. Sometimes Muslims and Christians will be speaking and acting in unfriendly environments, just as Jesus and the Prophet Muhammad did. They must be prepared to overcome prejudice against Islam and against Christians acting in concert with Muslims.

They must also be prepared to overcome prejudice against the very nature of their projects. Suppose a group of Christians and Muslims decides to address issues of poverty within their own local community. Poverty is not an accident. It is the product of unjust social structures created by vested interests and these vested interests will not take kindly to opposition or prophetic denunciation. The careers of both Jesus and Muhammad are testimony to this truth. The clearer Muslims and Christians are about their social justice purposes, the stronger their mission together will be.

Strong as the prejudice they will encounter may be, however, it cannot compete with two deeper truths: that the One God, the God of both Christians and Muslims, has particular care for those who are poor; and that this same God is identified in the scripture and traditions of both religions with justice.

A Shared Truth: The Option for the Poor

Consider the values that underlie these quotations:

> Then someone came to [Jesus] and said, "Teacher, what good deed must I do to have eternal life?" . . . Jesus said to him, "If you wish to be perfect, sell your possessions, and give the money to the poor, and you will have treasure in heaven; then come, follow me." When the young man heard this word, he went away grieving, for he had many possessions. (Matthew 19:16, 21–22)

> . . . and give generously of your possessions, for love of Him, to family, to orphans, to the needy, to the homeless, to those who ask; and pay the ransom for slaves; and observe proper worship and distribute a portion of your wealth to the poor. (*Sura al-Baqarah* 2:177)

The young man in Matthew's Gospel grieved at the loss of his possessions. But if he had been able to sell those possessions "for love of Him," as the Qur'an puts it, he would have rejoiced, not grieved.

To rejoice in giving to the poor "for love of Him" is exactly what is meant by the phrase "option for the poor." Sometimes the English form of the phrase creates misunderstanding. In the phrase's original Spanish form, *la opción para los pobres,* the word *opción* is much stronger than its English cognate *option. Opción* suggests that we *should* choose a certain thing, unlike *option,* which implies that we *may* choose it or not. The "option for the poor" refers to our moral obligation to put the needs of the poor and vulnerable first. But even more than an "obligation," the option for the poor is a key way in which we please God. And it is in pleasing God where we find the truest joy.

Pleasing God does not always mean that we are pleasing humankind, however. When the U.S. Catholic bishops noted that "Jesus takes the side of those most in need, physically and spiritually," they were well aware that his doing so put him on the side opposite those who are rich and powerful. The example of Jesus poses a number of challenges for Christians today, including defending those who are poor and defenseless, not by pretending to be their heroic saviors, but by seeing the world through their eyes, just as Jesus did. This is the only way to experience the power of God in the midst of poverty and powerlessness.[7]

A similar tension arises in Islam. Muslim scholar Farid Esack, himself a social justice activist during South Africa's struggle against apartheid, reminds us that the Prophet Muhammad made a personal choice to identify with those who were marginalized and poor. The Prophet even prayed to "continue living among the poor, to die among the poor and to be raised among the poor." Esack points out the inevitable result:

> The social and economic implications of the doctrine of *tauhid,* the idea that one Creator means a single humanity, were evident from the beginning of the prophetic mission.

At the heart of Muhammad's opponents' contempt was his lowly origin and his option for others from a similar background. The aristocracy of Mecca, with their commercially vested interests, were threatened both by his challenge to their traditional religion based on *shirk* and his emphasis on justice for the oppressed and marginalized.[8]

The treatment accorded the Prophet Muhammad recalls the resistance in high places that Jesus found as he identified with the marginal and oppressed of his day. In following Muhammad or Jesus, today's Muslims and Christians also need to place themselves among those who are poor and marginalized. But they are to do this in order to share joyfully in the struggle of the poor for justice, not to impose themselves upon the poor patronizingly.

Shared Truth Number Two: Identifying God with Justice

Among Islam's ninety-nine Beautiful Names for God is *al-'adl*, the Just One. Like all the Beautiful Names, *al-'adl* refers not to the inner essence of God (for that is unknowable), but to God's ongoing engagement with his creation. So "justice" is conceived of not as a noble but lifeless abstraction, but as God's ceaseless activity to establish and uphold right relationships among created beings. Many Qur'anic verses point to this divine activity. The dynamism of God's justice is the subject, for example, of the opening verses of one of the best-loved suras, namely, Sura ar-Rahman:

> The Most Merciful
> Has taught the Qur'an
> Has created human beings
> And taught them articulate speech
> Has placed sun and moon in their courses
> Plants and trees bow before him
> He has raised the heavens and set up the balance
> That you might not transgress it
> So establish weight with justice

That you will not disturb the balance
For he has spread out the earth for all his creatures. . . .
(Sura ar-Rahman 55:1–10)

These verses reveal that, for human beings, justice produces the balance that is foundational to creation as God intended it. All created objects maintain this balance naturally. For humanity, however, balance is not in-built as instinct but achieved as just action. The Qur'anic image uniting balance and justice evokes a merchant's scale where the weights are applied accurately and where each person receives his or her exact payment. The image, though a humble one, is also exalted since it bears witness to God's own creative activity: "And God has created the heavens and the earth according to a true measure [*bil haqq*]; and so that all may be justly paid for what they have earned and none be wronged" (Sura al-Jathiyah 45:22). Fair dealings become in this way acts of witness to God. To the extent that we engage in such dealings we experience that fairness in our turn.

By contrast, injustice upsets the balance and produces disorder and division. At the market place, weights are manipulated; the scales begin to lie; workers do not receive their due; impoverishment and exploitation of people and of the environment soon follow. "When confronted with this disturbance in the natural order through the systemic erosion of human rights (or threats to the ecosystem)," remarks Farid Esack, "the Qur'an imposes an obligation on the faithful to challenge such a system until it is eliminated and the order is once again restored to its natural state of justice."[9] The work of justice is not optional for Muslims. It is an obligation rooted in revelation and in the very nature of *al-'adl*, the Just One.

In the Jewish and Christian scriptures as well God is described as a "God of justice" (Isaiah 30:18). God demands justice from the whole people (Deuteronomy 16:20) and executes justice for the needy (Psalm 140:13). The U.S. Catholic bishops state that "central to the biblical presentation of justice is that the justice of a community is measured by its treatment of the powerless in society, most often described as the widow, the orphan, the poor, and the stranger (non-Israelite) in the land."[10]

The U.S. bishops point to the dual dimension of love of God and love of neighbor as the central theme of the covenant and the basis of the "Judaeo-Christian social ethic." (This ethic should now be understood as "Abrahamic," since Islam exhibits the dual dimension as surely as do Christianity and Judaism.)

> Biblical faith in general, and prophetic faith especially, insist that fidelity to the covenant joins obedience to God with reverence and concern for the neighbor. The biblical terms which best summarize this double dimension of Israel's faith are *sedaqah,* justice (also translated as righteousness), and *mishpat* (right judgment or justice embodied in a concrete act or deed). The biblical understanding of justice gives a fundamental perspective to our reflections on social and economic justice.[11]

Jesus takes on the prophetic tradition with its focus on justice for the oppressed in his inaugural address in the synagogue in his hometown of Nazareth. He reads from the prophet Isaiah, "the Spirit of the Lord is upon me, because he has anointed me to bring good news to the poor . . . release to the captives . . . sight to the blind . . . to let the oppressed go free." Then Jesus says, "Today this scripture has been fulfilled in your hearing" (Luke 4:18–22).

As Jesus and Muhammad discovered, the justice of God is not established without a struggle or controversy. The scene in Nazareth ends with the words: "When they heard this, all in the synagogue were filled with rage. They got up, drove him out of the town, and led him to the brow of the hill on which their town was built, so that they might hurl him off the cliff." For now, though, Jesus escaped the anger of the people: "But he passed through the midst of them and went on his way" (Luke 4:28–30). Struggle and controversy accompany those who seek God's justice. The three Abrahamic traditions acknowledge the necessity of struggle for God's disciples.

Jihad *for Justice*

In chapter 4 we linked the concept of *jihad* with peacemaking. Literally meaning "to struggle" or "exert oneself," *jihad,* we said, embraces a variety of meanings in the Qur'an. These include defensive warfare, moral self-discipline, exhortation, and contemplative spiritual struggle. But the concept has a further dimension. According to Esack, "the term *jihad* was always understood by Muslims to embrace a broader struggle to transform both oneself and society."[12] This is the dimension that allows us to equate *jihad* with the concept of "praxis" as used in Christian theologies of liberation. Both words refer to action that transforms society so that it will render justice for the oppressed. Esack himself makes the equivalence explicit: "one may say that *jihad* is simultaneously a struggle and a praxis." He goes on to quote Muslims in South Africa who worked to overturn the unjust system of apartheid. "*Jihad* is, therefore, a ceaseless, continuous, super conscious and effective struggle for justice."[13]

Jihad, praxis, struggle for justice — these terms denote action, but not action for its own sake. This action is a form of learning and knowing. Being engaged in the struggle for justice is a way of discovering the truth of the way social systems really work. The struggle for justice shapes our theoretical frameworks and our understanding of truth. "Praxis as a source of knowledge has always been widely recognized in Islamic scholarship and the Qur'an itself is explicit in its view that theory can be based on praxis: 'And to those who strive in our [path] to them we shall show our ways' (Sura al-'Ankabut 29:69)." The Qur'an emphasizes the importance of "correct praxis" known as orthopraxis and not only the importance of correct doctrine, known as orthodoxy. As Esack puts it: "The Qur'an lays great emphasis on orthopraxis and strongly suggests that virtuous deeds and *jihad* are also ways of understanding and knowing. The Qur'an establishes *jihad* as the path to establishing justice and praxis as the way of experiencing and comprehending truth."[14]

Christian liberation theology has made a similar point by reversing the traditional relation of action to theory. In older Christian theologies, theory came first; action was theory's servant. Then Peruvian theologian Gustavo Gutiérrez rearranged the relationship of theory and practice. He taught that theory (theology) is what you do when the sun goes down — after a full day of action on behalf of justice. "First is the commitment to charity, of service. Theology comes afterward; it is the second act."[15] According to American theologian Francis Fiorenza, "practice is no longer merely the aftermath of theory so that practice reflexively flows from theory. Instead practice is a source of experience that affects theory and influences how we interpret the world and our tradition."[16] In this approach, our action on behalf of justice actually shapes our theology and our understanding of truth.

The interplay of theory and practice unfolds in a number of different ways, including those cited below.

1. *Praxis opens up the text and the teachings of our traditions.* In light of our engagement in praxis we understand the meaning of the Bible or the Qur'an in new ways. One of this book's authors remembers hearing the Beatitudes in a new way when they were read in Rome by the Missionaries of Charity (a women's religious order founded by Mother Teresa) at a liturgy with the poor. He (one of this book's authors) had worked with the sisters in caring for the homeless of Rome. When the presider proclaimed, "Blessed are the poor," he had a new appreciation that this blessing was not meant just for the next life, but was a blessing right here and now in this community that cared for the poor.

2. *Praxis shapes the teaching of our traditions.* The text and teachings must be taught in a way that connects with reality and the current situation. Action on behalf of justice gives us that connection to reality and helps us explain the teaching. But our praxis can also lead to reshaping the teaching. The change in the Catholic Church's teaching on the death penalty reflects the effect of praxis. When the practice of sentencing violent offenders to life with parole became an acceptable option, the church altered its teaching to say that this "bloodless option" was a more ethical

way to protect society than was putting to death the offender. This change was brought about by many advocates working for the abolition of the death penalty.

3. *Praxis gives credibility to our faith.* On the personal level, comments Catholic theologian Roger Haight, "one can only . . . really know or believe something important in the measure that it bears fruit in action." Correspondingly, on the social level, "corporate praxis becomes the criterion of authentic witness." Haight continues: "Because authority lies in praxis, witness without praxis is not credible."[17] The Letter of James in the Christian scriptures makes the same point in down-to-earth, forceful language:

> What good is it, my brothers and sisters, if you say you have faith but do not have works? Can faith save you? If a brother or sister is naked and lacks daily food, one of you says to them, "Go in peace; keep warm and eat your fill," and yet you do not supply their bodily needs, what is the good of that? So faith by itself, if it has not works, is dead. (2:14–17)

Christian and Muslim traditions also reveal that God works with our human efforts to restore the balance of justice. The Qur'an teaches: "God does not change the conditions of a people until they change what is in themselves" (Sura al-R'ad 13:11). St. Paul reminds us that our work is required before God will intervene: "I planted, Apollos watered, but God gave the growth" (1 Cor. 3:6). This is not to imply that human efforts are in any way equivalent to God's, or that God, helpless to initiate justice, must wait on humankind's first move. It is to say that God demands initiative from us according to the strengths that God Himself has bestowed upon us.

And once we take those initiatives, our understanding of ourselves and of our world begins to change. Farid Esack concurs from his perspective that "both faith and understanding take shape in the concrete programmes of resistance against suffering and dehumanization."[18] In short, our understanding of God, our understanding of ourselves, and our understanding of our world are transformed when we engage in praxis, that is, in action on behalf of justice.

"Public Theology": Themes of Catholic Social Teaching

In addition to the clear evidence of the Bible on the importance of love of neighbor and the works of justice, Catholic social teaching has developed principles to guide a universal response to social issues. These themes were developed in terms of our common humanity and are not dependent on a specific faith allegiance. This is part of a "public theology" that invites conversation and collaboration in the secular and interfaith community. A few years ago one of us shared these principles with Muslim leaders and imams from various countries in Southeast Asia. One of the imams came up to him after his presentation and said that as a Muslim he could accept these principles.

Below is a list of these themes followed by corresponding principles from the Muslim tradition.

Theme One: The Human Dignity of All

The core value of Catholic social teaching is the *value and dignity of each person*. Human life is sacred from womb to tomb. Every life is of value, even the lives of those who commit grave evils, like murderers and even terrorists. Accordingly, any direct targeting of civilians in war or in retaliation for terrorist attacks is always wrong. The bishops state: "We believe that every person is precious, that people are more important than things, and that the measure of every human institution is whether it threatens of enhances the life and dignity of the human person."[19]

Muslim tradition is correspondingly strong in valuing human life. Qur'an Sura al-Ma'idah 5:32 states: "Anyone who kills another (except in punishment for murder or for spreading corruption on the earth) — it is as if he killed all humankind; while the one who saves a life, it is as if he saved all humankind." Even for murderers the Qur'an elsewhere holds out the promise that timely repentance will gain them reward in the life to come.

Theme Two: The Common Good

People are sacred and they are *social*. This principle leads to an emphasis on working together in community, strengthening families, and promoting the participation of all people *to work for the common good and the well-being of all,* especially those who are poor and vulnerable.

Muslim tradition emphasizes the common good just as strongly. The Prophet Muhammad's Farewell Sermon to the Muslim community gathered at Mecca — the sermon delivered just two months before his death in 632 — is full of prescriptions for just communal behavior. Among the social evils the Prophet warns against are usury, the abuse of women, and racism. "All humankind is from Adam and Eve," the Prophet declared. "An Arab has no superiority over a non-Arab nor has a non-Arab any superiority over an Arab; also a white has no superiority over a black or a black over a white except by piety and good action."

Theme Three: The Importance of Community

We will build healthy communities and achieve the common good when *human rights are protected and individuals take up their responsibilities to the community.* This is a two-way street: we have the right to the necessities of life and personal freedom, but we also have a duty to fulfill our responsibilities to ourselves, to our families, and to our communities.

Again, Muslim tradition everywhere asserts the link between rights and responsibilities. No better example of that linkage can be found than in the Prophet's earnest advocacy during the Farewell Sermon of the Five Pillars, where for the last time he urged the community "to worship God, say your five daily prayers (*salat*), fast during the month of Ramadan, and give your wealth in *zakat*. Perform *hajj* if you can afford to." Personal freedom unfolds in balance with a community that can nourish it.

Theme Four: Respect Human Rights

The common good means that the *dignity of work and workers' rights* must be recognized and protected. This principle entails various rights: the right to productive work, the right to a living wage, the right to join a union, the right to take economic initiatives, and the right to own private property. These rights are based on the assumption that the economy must serve people, and not that people must serve the economy.

The Prophet's warning against usury mentioned above runs through Muslim tradition as a red flag against the economic exploitation of the rich by the poor. "O People, just as you regard this month, this day, this city as sacred, so regard the life and property of every Muslim as a sacred trust. Return the goods entrusted to you to their rightful owners. Hurt no one so that no one may hurt you." In cases where a person's property has become dangerously depleted, *zakat* (alms) is the corrective.

Theme Five: The Need for Solidarity

Human beings are sacred and social, which means that *the human family is one.* We are our brothers' and sisters' keepers. Love of neighbor means loving our global neighbors. This is the principle and virtue of *solidarity,* which looks beyond religious, national, racial, ethnic, economic, and ideological differences to see the unity of the human family and our responsibility for one another.

We have heard the Prophet declare, "All humankind is from Adam and Eve." Only the quality of our deeds distinguishes us in God's eyes.

Theme Six: The Option for the Poor

As mentioned above, this element of "public theology," known as "the option for the poor," places *the needs of the poor and vulnerable at the center of our work for justice.*

For the Muslim tradition, too, a community's treatment of the poor and vulnerable among it is the measure of its commitment to the worship of God and to the love of neighbor.

A community commanded to follow the Farewell Sermon's "neither inflict nor suffer any iniquity" cannot tolerate within it any who have been abandoned or marginalized. "Remember that you will indeed meet your Lord," the Prophet solemnly intones, "and that He will indeed reckon your deeds."

Theme Seven: Respect for Creation

Finally, we show our respect for God by *respecting and caring for God's creation.* "We are called to protect people and the planet, living our faith in relationship with all of God's creation."[20]

Environmentalism as an explicit aspect of a life of faith is a modern understanding. Yet the principle can be inferred just as easily from the Muslim and Christian traditions. Take the following verse from Sura an-Nur 24:41: "Don't you see that it is God whom all beings in the heavens and on earth celebrate, even birds on outstretched wing? For each created thing understands its special way of prayer, and God is aware of all that they do." Prayerful meditation on such a verse quickly leads to respect and caring for a creation as equally centered on God as we humans are.

These seven themes lift out a few "starting points" for a comprehensive social ethic equally incumbent upon Christians and Muslims. Indeed, they give the broad lines of a public theology that is open to all people interested in serving the global common good and the survival of the good earth. But certainly to Christians and Muslims they provide an ethical horizon from which to view the complex social issues and needs before them. These themes will serve as both starting points for Muslim-Christian *jihad,* or praxis, and will be revised in light of that *jihad,* or praxis.

And it is to *jihad* or praxis that we now turn.

Discussion Questions

1. What did you learn about the common foundation of Islam and Christianity from the "Common Word" document?

2. Social justice is central to Islam and Christianity. What are the implications of this fact for their collaborative "action" in the neighborhood, community, nation, and world?

3. What are the implications of the statement, "Theology is what you do when the sun goes down"?

4. How does praxis open up, shape, and authenticate the teachings of Christianity and Islam?

5. Catholic social teaching offers seven "starting points" for a public theology. Which one grabs your attention and your heart? Explain why.

Chapter 8

LEAVING THE TENT

Theirs was no casual meeting. Francis and Malik al-Kamil spent days together, during a time of highest tension, on a battlefield already layered with dead from both sides. They met as representatives of opposed forces in a mighty world struggle for political, economic, and religious supremacy. Could the visit of Francis somehow break the bloody logic of events? The prospects for the peace both longed for were dim at best, and both must have suspected that their meeting could do little to alter that gloomy picture.

Yet as hopeless as the situation might have seemed to them, the conversation of Francis and al-Malik opened up possibilities for a very different way of relating, a way based on what today we call nonviolence. Personal inclination made this way attractive to them. So did good sense. The terms of the Sultan's offer of peace — the Crusaders' retreat from Damietta in exchange for the return of Jerusalem — offered a solution both knew should have satisfied the Christian side if it had not already committed itself to a zero-sum outcome. Finally, and most significantly, their faiths guided them to nonviolence. Both recognized that nonviolence was at the core of their religions' commandment to love God and neighbor. So whatever their heads told them about the uselessness of even talking about peace at such a time, their hearts said something quite different. They followed their hearts.

And because they did so, they left their meeting changed men. At least we can say that this was true of Francis. Afterward he became more resolved than ever to uphold the supreme value of peacemaking. In addition, he displayed an extraordinary openness to the Sultan's religion as well as a personal affection for the

Sultan that bespeaks the deepest love of "enemy." The meeting with Malik al-Kamil gave Francis his chance to realize his goal of following Christ's steps of peaceful reconciliation with the Other. Francis made the most of that opportunity.

If the meeting does not appear to have had as clear and as dramatic an effect on the Sultan, the difference may lie in the two men's relative degrees of experience of the Other. The Sultan, as we pointed out in chapter 4, was already well acquainted with Christians. And while Francis's special qualities as peacemaker must have greatly impressed Malik al-Kamil, especially in contrast to the bellicosity of Bishop Pelagius and of other crusading prelates, he would have known that among some monks, at least, true openness could be found. The Qur'an itself assured him of that. And we remember that Malik al-Kamil had met at least one such monk prior to Francis's arrival at the tent near Damietta. For the Sultan, meeting a Christian such as Francis did not represent the supreme way of confirming his very vocation as a Muslim, as Francis's meeting with the Sultan confirmed Francis's need to "love the Enemy" in radical obedience to the words and example of Jesus Christ.

Post-Damietta: The Sultan

What we can say about the Sultan's behavior subsequent to Francis's visit is that it showed no slacking from the commitment to peacemaking that preceded it. If anything, the Sultan's commitment shone out even more brightly.

Here's why we say this.

Francis returned at last to the Christian camp probably bearing from the Sultan a renewed offer of a peace treaty. Once again Pelagius rejected it. Soon afterward, the Muslims, who had been under siege for weeks inside the Damietta stronghold, were no longer able to resist the invaders and yielded their refuge without a struggle. The victorious Christians found inside a gruesome spectacle of death and disease. A city of eighty thousand had been reduced to three thousand starving souls. The army of Crusaders, having promised that survivors could leave with whatever belongings they could carry, reneged on their oath and "raped women in the night and massacred the inhabitants at will."[1]

What was Malik al-Kamil doing in his camp while this disaster unfolded inside the city? He was preoccupied and looking in another direction. He had just been told of yet another invading army, an even fiercer one than the army of the Crusaders: the Mongol hordes under Genghis Khan pressing on Muslim lands from the east. Bishop Pelagius triumphed when he heard the same news, calling Genghis "the executor of divine vengeance."[2] Pelagius resolved to take advantage of what he imagined would be the Sultan's resulting confusion and panic by launching an all-out attack directly on the Sultan's army.

Malik Al-Kamil did not panic. Instead, he renewed his peace offer. Once again Pelagius rejected it. During a lull in the fighting Malik al-Kamil made his offer one last time. Pelagius's final rejection proved fatal when the Sultan's armies routed the Christian invaders. But instead of annihilating his enemies when he had them cornered, the Sultan made sure they were treated well and given safe passage out of Egypt. The Crusader historian, Oliver of Paderborn, fulsomely praised the charity of the man James of Vitry had called "that cruel beast":

> The Sultan was moved by such compassion toward us that for many days he freely revived and refreshed our whole multitude. . . . Who could doubt that such kindness, mildness, and mercy proceeded from God? Those whose parents, sons, and daughters, brothers and sisters we killed with various tortures, whose property we scattered or whom we cast naked from their dwellings, refreshed us with their own food as we were dying of hunger, although we were in their dominion and power.[3]

The commitment to peacemaking Malik al-Kamil showed throughout the Fifth Crusade did not exhaust itself there. It came into play again after Pope Honorius III, stung by the Crusaders' defeat at Damietta, determined to launch yet another Crusade. Its chances for success seemed certain since it was to be led by the brilliant Holy Roman Emperor Frederick II. Frederick's armies set sail in September 1227, determined to take back Jerusalem. Yet their determination was sapped by the conflict that broke out between Frederick and the new pope, Gregory IX, who called off the Crusade to spite Frederick. The emperor, defying the pope, proceeded east. Yet knowing he lacked the necessary troops and fascinated by Malik al-Kamil's religion and culture, Frederick, instead of fighting to reclaim Jerusalem, regained it peacefully through the treaty he and Malik al-Kamil signed at Jaffa on February 11, 1229. The two men became friends. Frederick wept at Malik al-Malik's death in 1238. Like Francis, Frederick had crossed over and past the bloody battlefield of Crusader ideology and by doing so had learned to love his Enemy.

Post-Damietta: Francis

The Sultan's direct influence on Francis is easier to chart.

The struggle with the Crusaders having turned out in his favor, the Sultan did not forget his friend Francis. He gave him the right to preach to Muslims as well as free passage to visit the Christian holy places in Jerusalem. But Francis did not jump at these offers, as he would certainly have done earlier. He was ill. And he had gotten bad news from home. The nature of his Order was being changed in his absence. The Friars were acquiring property, and much was being made at home of the recent martyrdom of five young Franciscans who had provoked and received martyrdom in Morocco. Their aggressive, confrontational style of evangelization fit the church's ethos far more closely than the peacemaking approach of Francis.

Francis hastened home as quickly as he could. But he failed in his efforts to revive in his companions the love of Lady Poverty he had instilled in them. Too ill to return to Egypt, he wrote *A Letter to the Rulers of the People* in which he urged all those in authority to repent of their sins, especially those of avarice and bigotry that had led to the Crusades. Then he added an extraordinary instruction: "See to it that God is held in reverence among your subjects; every evening, at a signal given by a herald or in some other way, praise and thanks should be given to the Lord God Almighty by all the people."[4]

Paul Moses comments as follows on this instruction:

> Francis was obviously taken by the *adhan,* the call that he heard when soldiers in the sultan's camp were summoned five times a day to turn toward Mecca in prayer. He was not content simply to admire this practice; he wanted to bring that same intensity of devotion to the Christian world.[5]

Insistent that the instruction be carried out, Francis added: "If you refuse to see to this, you can be sure that you will be held to account for it at the Day of Judgment before Jesus Christ, your Lord and God."[6]

What impressed Francis about the *adhan* was its public and universal nature. To bow in prayer to God regularly throughout the day wasn't the work of religious communities alone. It was the work of the whole community, man, woman, and child, rich and poor, ruler and ruled, in a visible and physical sign of their allegiance to the One God. Francis thought that if such a rule could be instilled among Christians, their violent tendencies could at least be restrained.

Perhaps what kept the memory of the *adhan* fresh in his mind was the horn the Sultan had given him as a farewell gift, the only gift Francis accepted from the offerings the Sultan lavished upon him. Perhaps Francis wanted this tangible symbol of the importance of public, universal prayer in order to make his case for such prayer among Christians.

Yet whatever importance the horn held for Francis, it held none for many of Francis's brothers. *A Letter to the Rulers of the People,* along with other letters containing similar instructions, was suppressed by Francis's Order and lay buried for centuries.

We have already spoken (chapter 6) about a similar suppression, of Francis's 1221 *Earlier Rule,* in which he had urged those brothers undertaking evangelization in Muslim lands to "to avoid quarrels or disputes and to be subject to every human creature for God's sake." Fighting for its very life, the new Franciscan Order could not afford to listen to such language from its founder, especially at a time when the church was calling for a new Crusade, one that would overcome the shame of Pelagius's defeat at Damietta.

Franciscan Father Michael Cusato believes that, hearing news of this new Crusade, Francis was led to enter into the retreat at which he received the stigmata, the five wounds to his hands, feet, and side in sympathy with the wounds Christ had received on his cross.[7] Also during the retreat he wrote a prayer that strongly recalls the Muslim meditation on the *asma Allah-ul-husna,* the Beautiful Names of God. On the parchment's bottom he drew a figure of a head wearing a turban, along with words Father Cusato interprets as "I am weeping for you." Words and picture represent, in Father Cusato's view, an anguished prayer for Sultan al-Malik's well-being as the storms of yet another Crusade began to form around him.[8]

Concern for the Sultan wasn't the only source of anxiety for Francis. Strife and conflict surrounded him. In response, he did all he could to praise God's good creation and to celebrate peacemaking. Sick as he was, and soon to die, he wrote *The Canticle of the Sun,* adding a final verse to urge peace between the local bishop and Assisi's mayor:

> Praised be by you, my Lord,
> through those who give pardon by your love,
> and bear infirmity and tribulation.
> Blessed be those who endure in peace
> for by you, Most High, they shall be crowned.[9]

Francis died on October 3, 1226, one year before the armies of Frederick II set sail for the Holy Land.

Leaving the Tent of Meeting at Damietta

Prior to their meeting at Damietta neither Francis nor the Sultan had been disposed, as so many of their co-religionists were, to demonize the Other. Yet they still approached the Other cautiously and perhaps defensively, aware as they were of the warfare in which they were enmeshed and of the way in which religion had come to define and separate their respective "sides."

Their meeting enabled them to lay down their defenses and to open themselves to each other. Yet the meeting itself couldn't be the be-all and end-all. It couldn't remain a merely private miracle affecting only themselves. Francis and the Sultan were public persons, each in his own way carrying considerable authority in his respective religious and social sphere. How the two men related to each other at Damietta would affect many others. Both must certainly have been conscious of this fact. In Francis's case, we've seen how his Damietta experience led him to attempt to institute new prayer practices for his Order and to imagine a very different way for them to approach Muslims (and by implication to approach worshipers of other religions as well) than the aggressive ones then advocated and practiced. For the Sultan, the meeting may have increased his zeal to reach a treaty of peace with his Christian adversaries, a goal he eventually achieved with Frederick II.

Despite their many differences, they had found in each other the confidence and the inspiration that led them, as they departed their tent of meeting, to model peaceful interfaith relations ever more faithfully and creatively. Though their religions and cultures were still "at war" with each other, Francis and Sultan Malik al-Kamil worked hard not only to lessen the tensions between them but also to build new communities of trust. Francis and the Sultan now served the common good; their side's triumph over the Other was no longer their aim, if it ever had been.

Yet when Francis left the Sultan's tent at Damietta, he did not find himself walking on a yellow-brick road to Oz. His time with the Sultan had been transformative for him. But it had not magically changed the landscape of battle over which he had originally picked his way. He knew the implacable nature of Bishop Pelagius. He knew how deeply the crusading mentality had worked its way into the hearts of his co-religionists. If indeed he carried with him a further offer of peace from Malik al-Kamil, he could not have been hopeful that Pelagius would be more likely to accept it than he'd been before. Francis must have known that the broken ground over which he stumbled would soon be soaked again with blood.

Painful as that realization must have been for him, he was apparently spared knowledge, at least at this point, of a perhaps even more painful realization: the reshaping back home in Italy of his Order's mission. In his absence, Francis's advocacy for himself and his companions of a common life of radical poverty and peacemaking was being blunted in order to conform to the church's institutional needs. Those needs included advocacy of crusading and all that crusading entailed.

When Francis did discover what had been going on back home, he had to absorb disappointment and feelings of betrayal. His commitment to nonviolence was further tested by this implicit repudiation of the vision he felt the risen Christ had communicated to him. The offense done him was done to God. Yet Francis was obliged to respond as God's servant, not out of personal pique. And that response must itself be one of nonviolence.

As for the Sultan, he could no longer linger on happy memories of listening to and speaking with Francis. He had to prepare for the future battles likely to be forced on him by invaders: in Egypt against the Crusaders but also in the east against the Mongols. Somehow the Sultan had to maintain his commitment to peacemaking in a world that demanded from him just the opposite. Like Francis, he had to remain firm to his commitment to love God and neighbor in the most hostile circumstances.

Leaving the Damiettas of Today

Like Francis and the Sultan, Muslims and Christians gathering today to find common ground can't remain in their tent of meeting forever. Thankfully, they do not have to cross a literal battlefield in order to move out into the larger world. Yet in the United States, memories of September 11 remain vivid. Years of

Yellow Alerts and terrorist bombings, as well as ongoing wars in two Muslim-majority countries, keep battlefield imagery alive. The world in which Christians and Muslims are to join in solidarity is still disfigured by fear of the Other and by war. It will take courage for Muslims and Christians to subject relationships forged in intimate dialogue with each other to the incomprehension and possible hostility of those outside their circle. Francis's inability after his return to Italy to bring his brothers along with him on the road of poverty, peace, and reconciliation is a sobering reminder of how deeply entrenched fear of the Other is in us.

What's more, this fear takes different forms in different epochs. The way it manifested itself at the time of Francis and the Sultan is different from the way it manifests itself in today's liberal democracies, and especially here in the United States. Accurately assessing the present-day nature of this fear will be an important step Muslims and Christians working together will have to take. (We'll offer our own assessment at the end of this final chapter.)

Emerging from their tent, Muslims and Christians will first need to reach out to their respective co-religionists. Muslims will have to inspire Muslims, Christians Christians, with the force of the truth that they have discovered together, that the authentic expression of both their religions — necessarily setting aside theological differences and difference in worship — is their fidelity to their promise to love God and God's creation. Failing that, Muslims and Christians risk becoming reabsorbed into the selfish tribalism from which God called them.

Yet their efforts can't end with their co-religionists. God's prophetic commandment of love extends to all God's creation. It cannot be otherwise if God is One. Muslims and Christians leaving the tent of meeting have as their ultimate horizon the whole created world. Loving God and all God has made means that no one and nothing can be left out of the *salaam,* the fullness of life, which God intends all of creation to experience.

Preaching such a message isn't enough, however. Muslims and Christians leaving the tent of meeting are obliged to imagine and execute practical projects to enable God's creation to reach that *salaam*. And those projects must address the cries of those who have been excluded from the divine gifts of well-being that all must share. They must address those who are poor and marginalized.

But on what basis are such projects to be conceived? It is all well and good to talk in lofty generalities about helping the least fortunate. The real task is to know how that help can best be directed.

Toward Praxis, Toward *Jihad*

With some understanding of our common ground as members of the Abrahamic tradition and its focus on the Great Command to love God and neighbor, we move to the challenge of living out that tradition in a common work of service and social justice. We begin by providing guidelines for a group of Muslims and Christians planning to take action together.

Christians and Muslims who have previously engaged in social justice projects within their own communities may notice similarities between these guidelines and those they have seen and used before. This should not cause surprise. The practical aspects of developing social justice projects tend to be universal. What is special here is that this time it is Muslims and Christians who are following the guidelines. Those who believe Islam to be a religion of violence will be astonished to see Muslims working for social justice. They will be astonished further to see Muslims working on such projects shoulder-to-shoulder with Christians. In such a context, the symbolic value of the group's social justice work will be inestimable. Their actions will speak louder than words for the importance of interfaith cooperation.

Given this potential for their praxis to overcome or at least silence anti-Muslim fear, the group will do well to publicize their projects judiciously. Members of the group should not be shy about notifying local news outlets of their social justice work. They should invite members of the greater community to observe that work and to ask questions about it, as well as about the group's reasons for undertaking it together. Symbolic witness of this kind can become a potent tool both in overcoming fears and for stimulating others of either faith — or of different faiths or of no faith — to join in. After all, no one can be left out of the *salaam* intended for every one of God's creatures.

Guidelines for Common Praxis

Listening and Hearing

Listening and hearing are the first steps in the group's move toward action. Members have to be able to listen carefully, undefensively, and openly to the stirrings of their own hearts and to the stirrings of the hearts of those who are poor. Members show by this that they are truly hearing what they have listened to. What needs does the group hear articulated by those who are poor? Where does the group's passion for justice intersect with those needs?

But there is a prior question to be asked: Where should the listening to those who are poor begin? Will the group choose to meet with:

- farm workers caught up in the broken immigration system as they struggle to earn a living to support their families in Mexico and Central America?

- men and women returning home from prison hoping to begin a new life yet facing many obstacles and little support as they look for housing, employment, and a sense of belonging?

- refugees being resettled in our communities because of violence and persecution in their homeland?

- those living in poverty in our city and in our rural areas?

- those seeking safe and affordable housing?

- the elderly who may be isolated and struggling to stay in their own homes?

- children in need of mentoring?

- those who are homeless and hungry?

The group will want to spend some time discerning the focus for action. They may want to work on a project that members of the group are already connected with. Or they may want to undertake a new project. The project could involve a "one time" experience of collecting winter coats; or it could involve a long-term project extending over a number of months, even years. Perhaps the group will decide to listen to representatives advocating a variety of issues. Perhaps the group will do a few "site" visits before deciding on a course of action.

Yet while the project itself is important, equally important are the relationships that are being established within the group and with those the group hopes to serve. This sensitivity to others may mean that in picking an issue or a methodology members will choose an approach that all are comfortable with rather than one that may have a higher impact on the issue. In any case, members will keep in mind the three desired outcomes of loving our neighbor in action:

+ building relationships within interfaith groups,

+ learning more about the realities of those who are poor, and

+ creating conditions so that those who are poor can flourish.

Starting Out

Once it has chosen a focus, the group will meet with people affected by the chosen issue to gain a deeper understanding of these people's lives and the obstacles they face. Perhaps the greatest gift the group can give to those in need is to listen to their concerns and offer to build a relationship of trust. Members will have to "hold back" on their natural desire to "fix" people's problems. The first challenge is to meet them as equals in order to get an honest, unedited picture of their concerns, hopes, and struggles. Gaining this insight may mean, for example, sharing a meal with immigrant workers and beginning to see the world through their eyes. Or it may mean hearing the stories of ex-offenders who are trying to reconnect with the community.

Frankness should be met and nourished by frankness. The group's members should not only expect but even eagerly hope for questions about themselves and their solidarity with each other from their new friends among migrants or ex-offenders. Mutual frankness may lead to surprising moments of openness in which the value of interfaith cooperation can become real for everyone.

In their listening and hearing, the group's members will notice immediate needs that could be addressed. Perhaps the elderly could use help in fixing a broken screen door or they may simply need a ride to the grocery store or pharmacy. If members decide to assist those who are hungry, they will, no doubt, find themselves helping at a soup kitchen. This is important work. But they may want to go beyond meeting immediate needs.

Often those who serve meals at a soup kitchen do not really have the opportunity to get to know the people they are serving. For example, members may find themselves confined behind the serving counter. The group may look for ways of connecting at a deeper level than that of distributing the food they have prepared. Can they find more tangible ways of breaking down the barriers that exist between the "haves" and "have nots"? What opportunities might there be for the group to have meaningful conversations with their dinner guests? Would the offer to provide help in filling out social service forms and other paperwork be one of the services that could bring them in closer contact with the guests and at the same time answer the guests' real and immediate needs?

At the same time, the group will have to be sensitive to the wishes of the people they are serving who may not choose to share their stories. Members should seek out those who are willing to talk about their situation. They should respect the privacy of those who aren't.

An interfaith group would do well to connect with an established ministry that has built up relationships and trust with those who are poor. The leaders of an established ministry can be the group's guides and interpreters as members meet with people whose experiences are very different from their own. For example, the meal program at Blessed Sacrament Church in Rochester, New York, has added an extra dimension to the serving of suppers. Once a week a group of volunteers is available to help the guests with the "next steps" in their lives. These volunteers meet with the guests after the meal to help them with other specific needs, such as filling out welfare forms and connecting them with other resources in the community. Partnering with these trained volunteers would be a good way for the group to learn more about the guests who come for the meals and to hear about the obstacles they face personally and with the institutions in society. Partnering would also open up occasions of interfaith exchange between the group's members and the members of the ministry team assisting them.

Immediate Needs and Long-term Issues

As the group responds to people's *immediate needs,* they must be willing to listen for the *deeper issues,* such as the causes of people's homelessness, of their unstable refugee status, of their hunger, of their vulnerability as migrant workers. What obstacles do they face as they seek to improve their situation? Are there policies of the Department of Social Services or of Homeland Security or of state and federal legislative bodies that put obstacles in the way of their getting the help they need? For example, are there policies at the state level that make it more difficult for an ex-offender to find housing or a job?

As the group discovers these obstacles they may choose to become an *advocate for the individual* struggling to work through a particular difficulty. But group members may also want to address the policy itself so that others will not face the same or similar challenges. They can be both *advocates for the individuals* they are serving as well as *advocates who focus on the policy* that needs revision. Both types of advocacy are important and demanding. The group may move between individual and policy advocacy, or it may decide to concentrate on only one type of advocacy work.

For example, in working with migrant farm workers the group will see the workers' immediate needs for learning English and for obtaining better living conditions. The group may become an advocate for an individual farm worker who is facing obstacles or it may become an advocate addressing the practices, policies, and laws that limit or even threaten the farm worker's rights and opportunities. In many states farm workers do not enjoy the same protections under labor laws as other workers. This is true in New York State. In response, advocates for farm workers have been lobbying and educating state legislators for a number of years on these issues. Some advocates have worked with the farm workers so they can become their own advocates. They have taken Mexican migrant workers from western New York State to the state capitol to meet face-to-face with legislators. This ministry is called *empowerment* because those who are poor are empowered to speak for themselves. This type of social ministry enhances the dignity of the poor in that they become agents of change themselves and are not merely the recipients of the charity and advocacy of others.

Empowerment can also involve *community organizing*. The community facing obstacles to obtaining justice receives guidance in organizing themselves to address the systemic issues besetting them. Collective bargaining and unions are other expressions of empowerment where the workers themselves are given the tools to address their needs and working conditions.

For Example: Feeding the Hungry

The previous discussion may leave group members feeling confused or overwhelmed by the ranges of actions that a group can take in answer to the imperative to "love our neighbor." Yes, group members may admit the value of having many ways of responding to the needs they see. At the same time, however, they may find the sheer scale of the possibilities to be a burden. A helpful way out of such a dilemma is to clarify the options a particular "action" suggests. As an example of such clarification, let's look at the action of feeding the hungry. How can this action be broken down into a step-by-step series of feasible responses?

The first response is to provide food for hungry people through food cupboards and meal programs. This *direct service* approach is very straightforward. Its results are easy to measure — how many food baskets were distributed, how many meals were served. This is a safe starting place.

The second response to feeding the hungry is to *work as an advocate* for the clients or guests as they address their ongoing needs for food and other necessities of life. This is what the Next Step program at Blessed Sacrament Church offers the guests at its meal program.

As we get to know the guests at the meal program we discover the systemic issues that make it difficult for them to provide for their dietary needs. This is a third response to feeding the hungry. Here we *address the systemic policies and practices* that affect the food needs of our neighbors. We might discover that the lack of grocery stores in poor communities translates into a lack of affordable and appealing fresh fruits and vegetables. Or we may see the need for the expansion of food stamps and other subsidies to those who are poor. Systemic analysis of this sort will lead us to working with other coalitions and advocacy groups that are addressing these issues. Are there local groups, statewide groups, and national coalitions addressing hunger issues? What are the steps to partnering with them?

Finally, we may choose to work with *alternative models* of food production and food distribution to address the food needs of our communities. Community gardens in vacant city lots and church or mosque properties are examples of alternative models. Community Supported Agriculture (CSA) and local farmers' markets that establish a direct link between consumers and local farmers are other examples of alternative models that can respond to the needs of the poor in the community. The Catholic Worker movement has connected the urban poor with farms in its seventy-year history.

At any point along this range of responses the group should be alert to opportunities for increasing interest in interfaith solidarity. The effectiveness of such outreach may be enhanced by its indirectness, or, better put, by the fact that interfaith solidarity is in the group's case lived rather than preached (or preached by being lived, in the spirit of St. Francis himself). Whether by guests in soup kitchens or by members of legislatures, members of the group will find themselves asked about their identity and mission. The questions will probably come spontaneously, and therefore unexpectedly. Members will need to be ready to respond to such questions as they occur. They should welcome them, however ill-informed they may be. They will need to fit their answers to the needs and capacities of a variety of people. Difficult as these challenges may be, members should keep in mind that each question represents the chance to present both Christianity and Islam as well as the bonds between them in a light entirely unfamiliar to their questioners. This light will be a healing one, not the glare of prejudice. This light will shine all the brighter for being fueled by good deeds.

Practical Do's and Don't's

Helpful as a sequence of responses such as we outlined above might be, groups could still become sidetracked or find their energies diminished by certain very commonly occurring errors. Here are a few practical suggestions to help groups avoid these traps. The list is in no particular order of importance.

1. *Get Engaged.* Don't fall victim to the problem of "paralysis by analysis." While social issues are complex, responding to people in need is not. While analysis and study are important, they are not substitutes for action. One social ministry committee at a suburban Catholic parish that studied a variety of social issues for two years never decided on what issue it would tackle. Eventually the leader of the group moved out of state and the committee still did not know where to start.

2. *Don't Reinvent the Wheel.* If your group has chosen an issue to work on and has listened to the needs of those affected by that issue, find a group that is already addressing that concern and work with them — if at all possible. Your community might not need another food cupboard. Be patient until you discover

the need that hasn't yet been met. You probably won't have to wait long.

3. *Think Strategically.* Take the time to think about how your group can have its greatest impact. That might mean working on one aspect (of a larger issue) that no one else is addressing, or it might mean joining forces with an existing group on the same issue in order to have a greater impact on that issue. It might mean seeing yourselves as catalysts for getting your churches and mosques involved in the issue rather than just your own small group.

4. *Set Reasonable Goals.* Establishing modest goals and meeting them helps a group to stay focused. It also avoids burnout and discouragement, and it provides a way of evaluating your progress. After a specific time frame, gather to evaluate your work and adjust your objectives. You may have the background and expertise now to set more ambitious goals.

5. *Take Time to Celebrate and Evaluate.* Social justice work is hard. Systems of injustice can seem gigantic and unassailable. Take time periodically to celebrate your collaboration and your accomplishments, however small they seem. Then, in a relaxed atmosphere, reflect on lessons learned and on any new obstacles that have emerged. Pray for God's guidance.

6. *Enjoy the Journey.* Give thanks to God for the journey of walking with members of another faith tradition in the service of the poor.

Surveying the Land Ahead

In scouting out the obstacles Muslims and Christians will face as they leave their tent at Damietta, we have repeatedly called attention to two main ones: anti-Muslim prejudice and suspicion about the basis of interfaith solidarity in what we have called praxis or *jihad.*

But there is an even more deeply rooted obstacle the group will have to face and overcome, especially in the U.S. context —

a lack of understanding of the full implications of the prophetic commandment itself, and even antipathy to it.

God's commandment that we love God and God alone and that we love our neighbor as ourselves has always flown in the face of people's inherent tribalism: our seemingly unquenchable tendency to draw the wagons around our own social group in defense against or in defiance of the Other.

The cultural history of the United States reveals a still further development (or disfigurement) of this tribal principle: individualism, the individual-become-tribe, the belief in the ultimacy of the untrammeled self. The political expression of this belief, extreme libertarianism, threatens any effort to reform government; it also endangers the very sustainability of human community of any kind, even that of libertarians themselves. To such groups Muslims and Christians working together for the common good therefore represent the deepest possible challenge, a challenge not simply to their views about Islam or Christianity (which many Christian libertarians view as a private affair between themselves and Jesus), but perhaps even more fundamentally to the very possibility of human society.

The struggle to return the world to a vision of the common good isn't one Christian and Muslim groups will face alone, however. Their prayer and study together will enable them to join forces with many others for whom the idea of human society built on fairness and respect for the dignity of each person is still very strong — and may (we fervently hope) get stronger as the world's challenges continue to grow: political and economic challenges, certainly, but also environmental ones. What the struggle's outcome will be no one can say. But Muslims and Christians are blessed with the certainty that God is merciful and will respond to a community who calls out to God for help. Muslims and Christians may have a special role to play in conveying to others the optimism that comes from faith in the One God.

Discussion Questions

1. The Sultan and Francis knew that God asked them to be peacemakers in a violent world. Each of them had limited success in achieving that goal. What does their experience tell you about the journey of nonviolence?

2. This book has identified Malik al-Kamil and Francis of Assisi as heroes of loving God and neighbor. Share examples of other heroes from your personal experience.

3. How will the interfaith action of serving the poor and working for social justice change the attitudes of fear and prejudice in your neighbors?

4. Which issue affecting the poor do you think is the best place for your interfaith group to begin in light of the suggestions of this chapter? Explain with some detail.

5. Why do you think listening to the poor tends to be a radical concept for many Americans, as if the poor somehow represent the dangerous Other? What are your thoughts about the power of listening to the poor and the Other?

NOTES

Preface

1. John Tolan, *Saint Francis and the Sultan: The Curious History of a Christian-Muslim Encounter* (New York: Oxford, 2009), 12.

2. Ibid., 4.

3. Ibid., 325.

4. Frank M. Rega, *St. Francis of Assisi and the Conversion of the Muslims* (Rockford, Ill.: TAN Books and Publishers, 2007).

5. Tolan, *Saint Francis and the Sultan,* 325.

Introduction

1. The Pew Research Center for the People and the Press, "Public Expresses Mixed Views of Islam, Mormonism," September 25, 2007, 4; www.pewforum.org.

2. Ibid., 6.

3. The Pew Forum on Religion & Public Life, "Prospects for Inter-Religious Understanding," March 22, 2006, 5; *http://pewforum.org/Muslim/Prospects-for-Inter-Religious-Understanding.aspx.*

4. The Pew Global Attitudes Project, "The Great Divide: How Westerners and Muslims View Each Other," June 22, 2006, 1.

5. See "A Common Word" at *www.acommonword.com.* For a PDF copy of the "Open Letter" see *http://ammanmessage.com/media/openLetter/english.pdf* (italics added).

6. Pope Benedict, "Welcoming Speech," *www.vatican.va.*

7. Ibid.

8. John L. Allen, Jr. "A Theologian-Pope Sidelines Theology," January 22, 2010; see John L. Allen's blog at *http://ncronline.org.*

9. The Pew Forum, "Prospects for Inter-Religious Understanding," 8.

10. Council on American-Islamic Relations, *American Muslim Voters: A Demographic Profile and Survey of Attitudes* (Washington, D.C.: Council on American-Islamic Relations, October 24, 2006), 12.

11. Here is how Levinas expresses his vision of what he believes dialogue ought to be: "Beyond dialogue, a new maturity and earnestness, a new gravity and a new patience... *insoluble problems* [Levinas's emphasis],... not in order to find some most-common-denominator platform, but because they have understood that in certain conflicts persuasion itself is violence and repression.

"Neither violence, nor guile, nor simple diplomacy, nor simple tact, nor pure tolerance, nor even simple sympathy, nor even simple friendship — that attitude before insoluble problems: What can it be? What can it contribute?

"What can it be? The presence of persons before a problem. Attention and vigilance: not to sleep until the end of time, perhaps. The presence of persons who, for once, do not fade away into words, get lost in technical questions, freeze up into institutions and structures. The presence in the full force of their irreplaceable dignity, in the full force of their inevitable responsibility for each other... the difficult working on oneself: to go toward the Other where he is truly other, in the radical contradiction of their alterity, that place from which, for an insufficiently mature soul, hatred flows naturally or is deduced with infallible logic" (*Alterity and Transcendence*, trans. Michael B. Smithy [New York: Columbia University Press, 1999], 88).

12. Pontifical Council for Inter-Religious Dialogue, "Dialogue and Proclamation," #42; see online at *www.vatican.va/roman_curia/pontifical_councils/interelg/documents/rc_pc_interelg_doc_19051991_dialogue-and-proclamatio_en.html.*

1. Finding Common Symbols

1. Quoted from Ingrid Mattson, *The Story of the Qur'an: Its History and Place in Muslim Life* (Malden, Mass.: Blackwell Publishing, 2008), 20.

3. The Fundamentals of Christian Social Justice

1. Leonardo Boff, *St. Francis: A Model for Human Liberation* (New York: Crossroad, 1982), 39.

2. Ibid., 35.

3. Paul Moses, *The Saint and the Sultan: The Crusades, Islam, and Francis of Assisi's Mission of Peace* (New York: Doubleday, 2009), 10.

4. Jim Wallis, *God's Politics: Why the Right Gets It Wrong and the Left Doesn't Get It* (San Francisco: HarperSanFrancisco, 2005), 212.

5. See John Coleman, *An American Strategic Theology* (New York: Paulist Press, 1982), 10.

6. John Donahue, "Biblical Perspectives on Justice," in *Faith That Does Justice,* ed. John Haughey (New York: Paulist Press, 1977), 69.

7. Gerhard von Rad, *Old Testament Theology,* vol. 1, trans. D. M. G. Stalker (New York: Harper and Bros., 1962), 370; quoted by Donahue, "Biblical Perspectives on Justice," 68.

8. Walter Brueggemann, *The Covenanted Self* (Minneapolis: Fortress Press, 1999), 49.

9. Ibid.

10. Luke Timothy Johnson, *Sharing Possessions: Mandate and Symbol of Faith* (Philadelphia: Fortress Press, 1981), 79.

11. Ibid.

12. Ibid., 49.

13. Ibid., 108.

14. Ibid., 128–29.

15. William Herzog, II, *Jesus, Justice, and the Reign of God: A Ministry of Liberation* (Louisville: Westminster John Knox Press, 2000), 142–43.

16. Richard Hays, *The Moral Vision of the New Testament* (New York: HarperCollins, 1996), 329–30.

17. Ibid., 331, 332; emphasis added.

18. Lisa Sowle Cahill, *Love Your Enemies: Discipleship, Pacifism, and Just War Theory* (Minneapolis: Fortress Press, 1944), 3.

19. William H. Shannon, ed., *Thomas Merton: Passion for Peace: The Social Essays* (New York: Crossroad, 1995), 3–4.

20. Ibid., 4.

21. Tarif Khalidi, *The Muslim Jesus: Sayings and Stories in Islamic Literature* (Cambridge, Mass.: Harvard University Press, 2001), no. 37, 73.

4. The Fundamentals of Islamic Social Justice

1. Paul Moses, *The Saint and the Sultan: The Crusades, Islam, and Francis of Assisi's Mission of Peace* (New York: Doubleday, 2009), 89.

2. Ibid., 129.

3. Fazlur Rahman, *Major Themes of the Qur'an* (Minneapolis: Biblioteca Islamica, 1989), 7.

5. The Blessings of Our Religious and Cultural Sharing

1. Paul Moses, *The Saint and the Sultan: The Crusades, Islam, and Francis of Assisi's Mission of Peace* (New York: Doubleday, 2009), 46.

2. Ibid., 74.

3. Sydney Griffiths, "Christianity and Islam in Historical Perspective: A Christian View," available online.

4. Fazlur Rahman, *Major Themes of the Qur'an* (Minneapolis: Biblioteca Islamica, 1989), 164.

5. Griffiths, "Christianity and Islam in Historical Perspective," 3.

6. Ibid., 4.

7. See *www.schillerinstitute.org/fid_97–01/013_andalusia.html.*

8. María Rosa Menocal, *The Ornament of the World: How Muslims, Jews and Christians Created a Culture of Tolerance in Medieval Spain* (New York: Little Brown, 2002), 12.

6. Confronting Our Demons: Sin as Exclusion

1. Quoted in Paul Moses, *The Saint and the Sultan: The Crusades, Islam, and Francis of Assisi's Mission of Peace* (New York: Doubleday, 2009), 163.

2. LifeWay report: *www.lifeway.com/article/170230/;* also *www.prweb.com/releases/LifeWay_Research/survey/prweb3342584.htm.* For the Pew Report see *http://pewforum.org/Public-Expresses-Mixed-Views-of-Islam-Mormonism.aspx.*

7. Common Ground, Common Action

1. Paul Moses, *The Saint and the Sultan: The Crusades, Islam, and Francis of Assisi's Mission of Peace* (New York: Doubleday, 2009), 129.

2. Ibid., 133.

3. Ibid., 147.

4. Pope Benedict XVI, "Faith, Reason, and the University: Memories and Reflections" (English translation of "Glaube, Vernunft und Universität: Erinnerungen und Reflexionen," speech delivered at the Aula Magna of the University of Regensburg, September 12, 2006); *www.vatican.va/holy_/father benedict_xvi/speeches/2006/september.*

5. The problematic quote is: "Show me just what Muhammad brought that was new and there you will find things only evil and inhuman, such as his command to spread by the sword the faith he preached."

6. See "A Common Word" at *www.acommonword.com.* For a PDF copy of the "Open Letter" see *http://ammanmessage.com/media/openLetter/english.pdf.*

7. National Conference of Catholic Bishops, *Economic Justice for All: Pastoral Letter on Catholic Social Teaching and the U.S. Economy* (Washington, D.C.: USCCB, 1986), no. 52.

8. Farid Esack, *Qur'an, Liberation and Pluralism: An Islamic Perspective of Interreligious Solidarity against Oppression* (Oxford: Oneworld Publications, 1997), 100, 101.

9. Ibid., 104.

10. *Economic Justice for All,* no. 38.

11. Ibid., no. 37.

12. Esack, *Qur'an, Liberation and Pluralism,* 107.

13. Ibid.

14. Ibid., 107–8.

15. Gustavo Gutiérrez, *A Theology of Liberation,* trans. and ed. Caridad Inda and John Eagleson (Maryknoll, NY: Orbis Books, 1973), 11. The first sentence is missing in the English translation.

16. Francis Fiorenza. "Church, Social Mission of," in *The New Dictionary of Catholic Social Thought,* ed. Judith Dwyer (Collegeville, Minn.: Michael Glazier/Liturgical Press, 1994), 153.

17. Roger Haight, "Praxis," in *The New Dictionary of Catholic Social Thought,* ed. Judith Dwyer (Collegeville, Minn.: Michael Glazier/Liturgical Press, 1994), 776.

18. Esack, *Qur'an, Liberation and Pluralism,* 108.

19. United States Conference of Catholic Bishops, *Themes from Catholic Social Teaching* (Washington, D.C.: USCCB, 2005).

20. Ibid.

8. Leaving the Tent

1. Paul Moses, *The Saint and the Sultan: The Crusades, Islam, and Francis of Assisi's Mission of Peace* (New York: Doubleday, 2009), 130.

2. Ibid., 167.

3. Ibid., 175.

4. Ibid., 160.

5. Ibid.

6. Ibid.

7. See ibid., 180.

8. Ibid., 182–84.

9. Ibid., 186.

SELECTED BIBLIOGRAPHY

Background Books on Christianity

Introductions to Christianity

Johnson, Luke Timothy. *The Creed: What Christians Believe and Why it Matters*. New York: Doubleday, 2005. Argues that the Creed is no mere list of propositions but the very dynamic center of Christian faith.

Lewis, C. S. *Mere Christianity*. San Francisco: HarperSanFrancsico, 2001. Written in 1943 to overcome the agnosticism of a secular culture, this introduction to Christianity identifies succinctly and memorably key elements of Christian faith.

Introduction to the New Testament

Brown, Raymond E. *An Introduction to the New Testament*. New York: Doubleday, 1997. A full, judicious, scholarly but very accessible introduction to the history of the New Testament canon (accepted books) as well as a helpful guide to understanding key sections and passages of the books themselves.

Translations of the Christian Bible

The Holy Bible: New Revised Standard Version (NRSV). New York and London: Oxford University Press, 1989. The best modern version, scholarly but accessible and ecumenical in spirit.

The King James Version. Available from multiple publishers. The classic English version (prepared for King James I of England in the early seventeenth century). Still much quoted and still used in worship by many Christian denominations.

On Jesus

Johnson, Luke Timothy. *The Real Jesus: The Misguided Quest for the Historical Jesus and the Truth of the Traditional Gospels.* New York: HarperSanFrancisco, 1996. Vigorously argues against efforts to reduce the center of Christian faith, Jesus, to only a historical figure.

On Christian Spirituality

Day, Dorothy. *The Long Loneliness: An Autobiography.* New York: HarperOne, 1996. Revealing the way Day's emerging spirituality transformed her life into a prophetic career of service to the marginalized.

Merton, Thomas. *New Seeds of Contemplation.* New York: New Directions, 1961. A passionate argument by a Trappist monk for the fulfillment of Christian faith in contemplation (oneness with God, leading to oneness with humankind).

Christian Social Teachings

DeBerri, Edward, and James Hug, eds. *Catholic Social Teaching: Our Best Kept Secret.* 4th ed. Maryknoll, N.Y.: Orbis Books, 2003. This updated version includes an outline of documents from Latin America, Africa, Asia, Australia, and Europe along with the classic papal, Vatican, and U.S. bishops' statements.

Evans, Bernard. *Lazarus at the Table: Catholics and Social Justice.* Collegeville, Minn.: Liturgical Press, 2006. A very readable, brief text written for those involved in social justice ministry that articulates the principles at the heart of Catholic social teaching.

Hollinger, Dennis. *Choosing the Good: Christian Ethics in a Complex World.* Grand Rapids, Mich.: Baker Book House, 2002. Provides a framework for understanding Christian ethics in a secular, pluralistic context.

Massaro, Thomas. *Living Justice: Catholic Social Teaching in Action.* Lanham, Md.: Rowman & Littlefield, 2008. An updated explanation of the key themes of Catholic social teaching.

Mich, Marvin L. Krier. *The Challenge and Spirituality of Catholic Social Teaching.* Louisville, Ky.: Sowers Books-JustFaith, 2005. A blend of biblical, theological, and spiritual insights on the seven themes of Catholic social teaching. Written for the JustFaith formation program.

Background Books on Islam

Overviews of Islam

Aslan, Reza. *No god but God: The Origins, Evolution, and Future of Islam.* New York: Random House, 2005. An introduction to Islam tracing the ways history and culture have influenced its development.

Dardess, George. *Meeting Islam: A Guide for Christians.* Brewster, Mass.: Paraclete Press, 2005. An introduction to Islam showing how Christians can strengthen their own faith through intimacy with Islam and with Muslims.

Nasr, Seyyed Hossein. *The Heart of Islam: Enduring Values for Humanity.* New York: HarperSanFrancisco, 2004. An introduction to Islam emphasizing Islam's support of values underlying all human flourishing.

Geopolitical Assessment of Islam

Graham E. Fuller, *A World without Islam.* New York: Little, Brown and Company, 2010. The writer, a former vice chairman of the National Intelligence Council at the CIA, argues that current tensions between the West and the East do not result from religious conflict with Islam, but with geopolitical power issues that would have occurred had the Prophet Muhammad never existed.

Introductions to the Qur'an

Dardess, George. *Do We Worship the Same God? The Bible and the Qur'an Compared.* Cincinnati: St. Anthony Messenger Press, 2006. Presents parallel passages on common themes from both scriptures in order to help readers decide whether Christians and Muslims do in fact worship the same God.

Sells, Michael. *Approaching the Qur'an: The Early Revelations.* Ashland, Ore.: White Cloud Press, 1999. Introduces the Qur'an's early suras (chapters) by presenting their extraordinary auditory and linguistic qualities. Includes a DVD with examples of Qur'an chanting.

Versions of the Qur'an

The Meanings of the Holy Qur'an. Trans. Abdullah Yusuf Ali. Available from multiple publishers. The English version perhaps most often cited. Reliable, but dated.

The Qur'an. Trans. M. A. S. Abdel Haleem. Oxford: Oxford University Press, 2004. Perhaps the best modern version. Contains an excellent introduction.

On the Prophet Muhammad

Safi, Omid. *Memories of Muhammad: Why the Prophet Matters.* New York: HarperOne, 2009. A biography of Muhammad that also evaluates how he has been loved — but also misunderstood — not only in the past but also in our own day.

On Islamic Spirituality

Rahman, Jamal. *The Fragrance of Faith: The Enlightened Heart of Islam.* Bath, U.K.: The Book Foundation, 2004. Beautifully written guide to the practice of Islamic spirituality.

Sells, Michael, ed. *Early Islamic Mysticism: Sufi, Qur'an, Mi'raj, Poetic, and Theological Writings.* Classics of Western Spirituality. Mahwah, N.J.: Paulist Press, 1996. An excellent compendium of the early foundational texts of Islamic spirituality. Contains helpful notes and introductions.